is

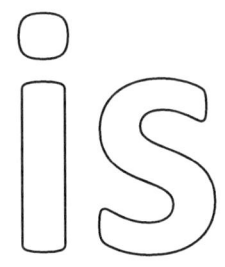

The Phenomenon of the Facebook Status

Patrick Hamilton Walsh

is: The Phenomenon of the Facebook Status

Copyright © 2009 Patrick Hamilton Walsh. All rights reserved. No part of this book may be reproduced or retransmitted in any form or by any means without the written permission of the publisher.

Published by Wheatmark®
610 East Delano Street, Suite 104
Tucson, Arizona 85705 U.S.A.
www.wheatmark.com

International Standard Book Number: 978-1-60494-229-3
Library of Congress Control Number: 2008943388

*To Johanna and Emma for their help and
to my family and friends for their unending love and support.*

Live. Laugh. Learn. Love.

Contents

Introduction 7

is full of lurve.. 9
is having the time of their life 11
is giving out way too much information 13
is living it up 15
is living it up ... way too much! 18
is feeling rather... 23
is spending too much time on Facebook 27
is struggling for a status update 31
is trying too hard.. 34
is doing that thing they get paid to do 35
is out of the country.. 40
is trying to rub it in 44
is a huge sports nut 47
is a huge football nut 50
is offering an insight... I think............................ 54
is wishing things were different............................. 55
is ... WTF?.. 58
is needing a big hug 62
is getting out of here 65
is reflecting 68
is loving themselves right now 70
is sticking it up there for all the world to see, you know, just in case... 74
is being cheeky 79
is going to have to make some changes 80
is starting to make changes 84
is currently living off savings 86
is trying to get this damn qualification 88
is living for the weekend 92
is celebrating the passing of another year 95

is just reminding you all 97
is talking about the weather … again! 98
is more than a little confused at the moment 101
is not saying much 104
is saying even less 108
is chillaxing 112
is thinking with their belly 114
is not having the most fun 118
is going to get fit 119
is a true backpacker 121
is actually enjoying the summer 124
is announcing to the world… 126
is boring 127
is counting the days away 129
is maybe a little obsessed with popular culture… 131
is making an observation 134
is thirsty 136
is needing some anger management classes 137
is obviously losing their mind 139

Facebook Facts 141

Introduction

In May 2007 I jacked in my job and set off from Dublin airport to see the world and live my life out of a backpack as a free man, away from the madness and the rat-race that is the Western world. Looking back to that time I feel it is fair to say that at that stage I was a bit of a laggard when it came to these new 'how-to-keep-in-contact thingies' like Bebo, MySpace, etc dismissing them as new techno-toys and fads of school kids.

But my opinion has changed! Based solely on the places I have visited and the people that I have met during my travels, it appears that throughout Ireland and Scotland Bebo has a large number of users, while MySpace is hugely popular in America. But over the past year, no matter where I have been in the world, from Texas to Tehran, from Calcutta to Kathmandu, from Sao Paulo to Sumatra, it seems like nearly everyone has a Facebook account. With over 100 million users worldwide Facebook is one of the world's fastest growing social networking sites, and I think it's fair to say that when it gets to the stage where people ask for Facebook account details to keep in contact instead of telephone numbers, that Facebook has become a phenomenon.

The attraction to Facebook is that it appeals to so many different people on so many different levels. Some people love the access it gives them to their friends photos, some like the way they can see at a glance from the live feed what their friends are up to, others enjoy the hundreds of applications that can prove how popular they are, etc but for me I always have a laugh out loud at what people have listed as their status. It can give the world (depending on their privacy settings) an insight into the person's soul and how they are feeling at that moment, in a way that nothing else ever has.

The interpretation of the status all depends on whether you are on that person's wave length, because what a person lists as their status may leave one person laughing until their belly hurts, can leave another cringing, while everyone else is totally confused as to what they are trying to say! So here it is, a book dedicated entirely to the *'is'*s that people may possibly list as their status.

For those of you not totally familiar with how the Facebook Status works here is a quick introduction:

The account holders name is listed at the top of the page with the word 'is' after it to encourage people to list what they are currently doing or their current thoughts. The person then can enter anything that they wish the world to know, for example, Patrick is wondering if this is the first book to have been written predominately in Internet Cafes.

Recent developments on Facebook allow the account holder to overwrite the word 'is' on the status bar to include anything they wish. An example of this would be, Patrick wants to thank you for all your support.

You are free to write anything that is on your mind within the status bar, but you are restricted to around 150 characters.

is full of lurve

is so in love with Kevin that she can't breathe. I'm so glad we met. Thanks to those who have accepted us being together.

is saying thank you so, so, so, so much Mr Spontaneous. I love you more than anything in the entire world.

is in the land of love.

finds out that her own story has a happy ending!

is back on her toadstool in the land of love.

loves his beautiful girl!

is very much looking forward to Monday night... you know who you are!

is in love... as always!

has a cheeky smile and only she knows why!

is saying you don't know what your doing to me with your love...

thinks the love is greater than they will ever know, it's deeper than the sea blue. You put a spell on me and you didn't even mean to.

is thinking words can't describe my love for you.

likes walking around with Stephen.

woke up early to enjoy more of the day :)

is in love with you.

likes to spoon Mia in bed.

is one happy little lady today!

had the funniest and most exciting night of his life with Aideen.

is loving the way things always work themselves out for the best... every single time!

says no matter what I do, I still love you.

is so in love with him.

loves her sister lots and lots.

is in love with Andrew and misses her shmoo so much.

says thanks babe, love you.

is glad Jonathan's here :)

thinks that work is shit, but is glad she is seeing a certain someone that will make her smile tonight.

is love; wrapped in the promise of a sunrise.

still can't stop smiling after her date on the weekend...!

is in love with his girlfriend.

has got her baby back!

is so happy to have her Nacim back especially because he looks as handsome as ever!

spent the day in glorious sunshine walking barefoot on the golden beaches of Great Yarmouth. All while in the company of a wonderful lady.

is finally getting Karl back!

has been blessed with the most amazing family ever!

is thanking the friend who is a boy...

caught some nice sun yesterday whilst spending six hours in some very interesting company, and thoroughly enjoyed it! He'll be doing it again very soon...

is very excited to be engaged!

is thinking about something which makes her happy ;-D

gives plenty of loving...

is currently having an amazing candle-lit dinner at Betsy's house!

can't wait for her lil ray of sunshine :)

is with Sonya again.

has got love for you, big love for you...

is loving life! Thanks to everyone who is contributing to that feeling! You know who you all are :-)

loves you Kay.

is pretty god damn happy right now...!

almost melted when she heard her 18 months old niece calling her 'RIA' for the first time!

is home and happy.

wants her boyfriend to know she loves him lots and lots!

is loving having mum here!

is glad to have her Alan back!

loves repeat, LOVES Daniella Jauregui!

is letting you know that you are my number one!

can't wait to see Ana and the doggies.

is thinking of someone!

says: if I hadn't of met you I wouldn't have fallen for you, but I did and I have, and there's nothing I can do.

is cuddling Ulrike for comfort.

is going to see her favourite Arab...

is having a "few" glasses of wine with her beautiful mum... I love her...

is thinking Alexandra is lovely (unlucky Jamie).

is loving all the mini dinner parties her friends keep holding and the flow of el vino!

loves this beautiful girl he calls his missus...

is really enjoying his last weekend, monkeying around, in absolutely fabulous and refreshing company.

is over the moon that Siobhan said yes to marry him.

is looking forward to a nice night in with her boyfriend! Love you babe.

is having the time of their life

thinks last night was unexpected and brilliant! Love you Laura!

is loving the parties on the Palm islands.

doesn't want this year to end.

is thinking one of the funniest things EVER happened last night, ha ha ha it was legendary... and it was caught on CCTV!

had an awesome night last night. Cheers heaps Amy, you're a real gorgeous girl!

is thinking... that's what I'm talking about!

owns a Les Paul... wicked!

is having one of those 'Thrill seeking Thursdays' with the BBC. Brilliant!

has actually had the best night ever... she loves Madelen, Matthew and Ida more than life.

is never going to forget the moments she had with Taio Cruz... ever, ever, ever!

can't stop laughing... love it!

is dancing emphatically and dreaming of South West 6.

never wants to go home… she's going to the gay pride Mardi Gras this weekend and maybe the Zoo too.

had the most amazing weekend! Wow, gonna be hard to beat!

is going to get fucking wasted tonight and get it on with a slag! Why? Because I'm on holiday and I can!

is merry making at my place.

has just got back from Space opening party… OMG is the only words I have at the minute!

is truly free, living the dream!

has had an amazing Friday with Aimee (although she is still feeling sick).

is happy. Just finished drafting a children's book, and going out for a meal for my birthday tomorrow with three of my favourite people.

is sitting at his desk drinking a beer. I love New Zealand.

has had the best bloody weekend ever! Why can't she have every weekend off!

is having a good night, every night.

had a great night and cannot bloody wait to toast myself in the south of France! yup yup!

is amazed at how things can change, loves everything at the moment, can't wait to go on holiday, and is officially addicted to heroes.

will live this one like it's the last.

had 35 people naked last night when playing my games… it was heaven… I knew I could do it.

is having fun talking shit to good friends!

thinks Brisbane rocks… and Krispy Kreme opens this week, and it's just around the corner from work…

is eagerly anticipating the madness that he and the hairy one will muster up this year :)

had one of the funniest weekends ever.

is living the dream…

arrived alive! Yay for Adelaide: best weekend ever even despite the stupid car trouble.

is loving the vibe from the weekend!

is living it large! He is in Australia living with two women dancers (and they're hot!).

has never laughed so much as he did last night. Rachel should write every incident report.

is once again surprised at how lucky he is…

has just been shopping and was bought a whole new wardrobe! Spoilt!

is loving the new additions to the Reading line up, and an exciting end to the football season, and the fact GTA's release coincides with the end of his exam!

is going to Pittsburgh to reunite with her SAS lover for the price of 45 Balboa cervezas. Life is good!

had such a fun day yesterday! When's the next one planned!

is loving life... bring on the next stage...

can't believe how lucky he is to be in such a place, surrounded with such outstanding people.

is just fresh from the Lambo garage and the Aston Martin garage... I have decided on the Vantage Coupe!

thinks life is actually incredible :)

is 21, single, and partying in Ibiza.

came second in a dance competition in Murphy's! Stupid arse judges! And to make it worse, it was my cousin of all people that beat me!

is wishing himself Happy Anniversary, one year of the grid, a free man nonetheless! All the people that have made me laugh over the past year... I love you still!

is giving out way too much information

is now finally a fully paid up member of the mile high club.

just got back from the Virgin Islands... now they're just called the Islands!

is so horny now after watching some on-line porn!

wonders would having an injury caused by sex make you a super stud or would it make you a learner in the bedroom?

is single and back on the hand-pump.

's penis is too small to see.

is itching in a certain place where it is not so nice... but I tell you, she looked so innocent!

is choking his chicken.

never knew how much fun she could have with a fat cucumber and a packet of chalk...

is gutted Andreas and Jens turned down anal... again.

is a member of the sex sex one group...

cant wait for next years Steak and Blowjob day already, as this year it was so good.

is doing some video work in the bedroom!

has a semi again!

is very proud of his c-men today.

is saying you know who you are… and you are just a wanking prick… you have destroyed my new sheets!

just finger banged your mom.

is really loving the Danish-Slag-Loves-American-Slag thing that is going on—How good can it get?

is an erotic freaking freak.

will loan you her toothbrush, she'll bartend your party. She will even give you a good…

is about to eat pillow.

thinks ANZAC Day is a truly wonderful thing… all those men in uniforms giving me naughty thoughts…

is having serious sp-orgasms—Sean Paul's got skills!

is not a fan of condoms.

is pushing his seed somewhere deep in her chest…

is saying have a read at this: 'hospital worker Pedro Gonzales surrendered to Miami police on Wednesday after police say he performed oral sex on male patient who was waking up from surgery.'

is going back, even after some black…

thinks the Ginge should've put out!

is loving his sex change! I can finally be the woman I've always wanted to be and suck all the cock!

is dirty, very dirty.

will never look at a penis the same way… neither would you after an hour of penis puppetry!

is doing it with a cosmopolitan in her hand!

is really getting into this S&M shit!

thinks Euan's wife is in for a corker tonight!

is apologising to Miss Wan King about the criticism of her technique last night!

is preparing for a sex party tonight.

can only taste latex and her hands smell of latex too…

is up for it… Red Light District here I come!

knows how to look good naked… STOP LAUGHING!

is just going to sit here all night with his good friend Charlie, and have a good time!

thinks that dogs should stick to bitches and get off my leg.

is sambucca'd out… it has turned black!

has a sore bum hole after a long 'ride' home.

is off until Monday! Get up them stairs you sexy minx!

has just wet herself!

is going to be much more specific next time she asks for a bikini wax. Pass me a large vodka please!

is making love to your face.

has been a very naughty little girl, and now her hand is all sticky.

is knocked out with his cock out.

sssshhhhhhh! Three times in one day. And on a Sunday too!

is proud to be one of the two official creators, and the current champion of erotic pool.

wants to be shagged up the arse; by a horse...

is going to a strip club tonight!

enjoys a nice finger up the bum.

is riding a white swan.

whoever suggested bed rest should be shot, it's so boring! Although I wouldn't mind so much if I had a certain man in my bed with me for some action. You know who you are!

is living it up

is drunk on life... and alcohol.

reckons that there is copious amounts of whiskey sitting at home that probably needs to be smashed... this long weekend seems like a relatively good opportunity to smash it!

is still trying to banish images of Sarah putting condoms up through her nose and out through her mouth from his mind!

is hoping that tonight is the night.

is loving Mardi Gras and the casino baby! :-)

is most likely drunk...

is cooking up a storm for uncle Paul and Maria tonight, and making them drink cocktails. Providing she can find some bloody tropical juice in this city!

is bar tending in Melbourne... bring on the booze for each and all.

is awake and up for Oz Fest!

is feeling a lot better today and ready for more champers in BA.

is having to get her groove on without her g****!

is stepping out in her sexy red shoes!

is having a slight hangover, but tonight is Queensnight and tomorrow is party hardy Queensday!

is thinking that Broadstairs should be visited again!

is so happy that she can finally go out this week.

says lil miss Giles and lil miss Hogget... y'all ready to crunk!?

is needing a happy pill for tonight. Or two!

is suffering after having a few pints last night and could not believe the size of her glass! A pint is huge!

is looking forward to seeing The Moscow Secret in London tonight.

is having a great day walking around watching people get drunk in honour of their Queen...

is mashedupinadance!

is going to Shapeshifters tonight and Pendulum on Saturday... going to be a messy weekend!

is unemployed and ready to partay!

wonders where people party on a Friday night these days?

is going solo this weekend...

had a messy night last night and is going out again tonight...

is enjoying the sounds of Iron Maiden before going out.

is the big beat manifesto!

had it large in my Dad's shed on Saturday night with Meat Loaf.

is recovering from an all day bender earlier.

is wondering who's in Londontown and available for a BBQ in north Acton this Saturday? All welcome!

is out tonight, what's people doing?

can't wait for skool disco @ Chicago's, Luton! People be there or be boring!

is going to be busy tonight for the long anticipated red eyed, feat. Dave Broughton and Mumford & Sons.

was at the Redback last night. Quite the experience!

is starting her weekend in Cordoba as she means to go on!

has got 110 in tonight... it's going to be big baby.

is going AWOL until Sunday.

is at Black Point for the weekend!

is making Aruba get ready for Electric Rush - Global Gathering 2008.

is going out tonight with good friends.

is on the big weekend's merry-go-round.

was going to do an all-nighter, then a half-nighter, then a quarter-nighter, then zzzzz in bed.

is fuck yeah splendour weekender.

is rockin' this party with Bob Sinclair... oh yeah!

is skint! Spent a lot more than expected at the strip club last night.

is on a drinking rampage tonight...

is in Dylan's room. Drinking blue stuff. Getting ready for a beach party!

is feeling the music so pump up the jam.

still has a sore back but might go out for a few cheeky ones later.

is rave in a cave, ooh my!

is ready to get his cast off because it's time to party... now with just a brace...

is smashed in Seaview!

parties for the right to fight and write on...

is out tonight celebrating!

is at the Velvet for the party night. It's good to be back!

is doing it all over again tonight...

is getting steaming tonight and staying up until 4.30am for the game.

is staying away from marching powder.

is fucked after doing a ten hour shift... Sunday sessions get better.

just got home from a wicked night with her Jew...

is having a pants party.

is loving Irish disco biscuits and is excited for Halloween!

is going out again! Surprise, surprise!

is having a month off the booze starting next Sunday! So look out on Saturday night fuckers!

dances like a menace to society when he's drunk...

is going to the city on a school night.

is dreading seeing the pictures from Saturday night!

is going fucking crazy tonight so get yourself down and party hard, we've got booze and everything.

is sticking to the floor.

is going out tonight with good friends.

is gonna be burnt out by 7am on Saturday morning… because it's Festiball.

is back in the room and ready to AFTER PARTY.

is up for going to every festival this summer!

is trying to marry Mary Poppins… and hitting the Font tonight, "who wud'av fort"…

is off to the West-fucking-End.

is home for the weekend, and getting hosed!

is going out tonight! He's going to get blind and get a big party going, oh yes.

is forever on the dancefloor…

is drinking again tonight… seek me people!

is on a bender!

needs another night out and is going to have it again soon.

is busting it out!

and Susan are in Sin City, living large!

is thinking he should really start getting ready for this big one!

had such a good night last night, is still singing "hey mama, hey mama!" and is wondering if the bus driver is dead?!

is off on a Saturday for the first time in ages, Aardvark, here we come…

is the smallest man in Ibiza, and is CHARGED!

is living it up … way too much!

honestly can't believe he is still alive after one of the craziest weekends ever…!

is yipikaye hung-over.

is thinking finishing the night with five B52's was not a good idea, he feels like shit!

is trying to recall who 'John 2' is on her phone… does she answer?

is thinking about emergency services!

was a touch out of control over the weekend!

is looking for her voice.

is thinking maybe last night wasn't such a good idea after all.

is smarter than you because he has found a cure for jet lag... stay up until midnight and get hammered.

is in serious need of a detox.

is tattooed to the couch nursing a hangover, watching David Icke live.

has the Sunday fear!

is recovering after last night! This Rose wine/Thursday night's thing is killing me!

is hung-over to fuck.

is very rough and getting worse as the hours pass...

is living a life of XS.

is never drinking beer again, even if it is from Cheshire.

is regretful after her beelaryness.

is very slowly recovering from the monstrous hangover (and sunburn) resulting from the wedding...

isn't feeling well... still, and is doing some soul searching!

has another hangover... STANDARD!

is as rough as a bears arse! Dam you cheap jugs of beer!

doesn't remember posing for her profile pic... hmmm.

is hung-over... but ready for round two tonight!

hopes somebody found her phone and shoes last night!

is quitting alcohol, I shit you not, I am quitting!

is trawling through the debris searching for survivors...

is recovering after having two nights out last night—the affects of such rash behaviour are taking effect.

is still ill thanks to someone - you know who you are!

is all Corona'd out.

is having trouble engaging his brain... again.

got Muhammad last night then couldn't afford to buy a kebab so ate a load of tuna instead... Mmm!

is monged clean out of it.

does not want to wake up tomorrow and face the week ahead.

is feeling very tired having drunk too much this week... bring on the weekend!

is truly needing to stop drinking!

doesn't know if spending half a night pissed is worth spending a whole day hung-over...

is wondering who, where, when? And, of course, WHY?

is gutted to have missed the bus to Napier. No, No, No, No. Why did I treat myself to those four dollar beverages?

is going to be having the red eye in work tomorrow after today's green eye!

has the hangover from hell and didn't make it in to work for a change.

...fucking hell we got pissed last night.

is half pissed again... and it's only Monday. This is not the way the week was supposed to start...

is feeling ill. A few too many Sambuccas last night!

is so over partying until Friday!

doesn't rate alcohol anymore...

is over the alcohol poisoning and is ready for a mad one in Wellington boot tonight!

is ready to give his liver a rest and head home to his bitch.

is completely off her head still.

doesn't have a hangover... yet... probably because she's still pissed!

is exhausted but still has more parties to go to...

reckons its time for bed now as it is 7am on Sunday morning.

is struggling to put sentences together.

can't remember a thing!

is thinking NO, NO, NO to red wine!

was a severe HOT MESS... cant believe I walked home on my own, steaming in the pissing down rain and made a point of stopping for 15 minutes to look for my keys.

is in recovery mode.

discovered ill recipes, without the ride on ecstasy...

is definitely burning the candle at both ends, but feels that he gives off more light that way.

is going to work after spending his day off drinking like hell!

is impressed with his drunken criminal abilities...

had the best scattered weekend, but it may have caught up on him and is feeling a bit down... sigh!

is unsure how he got from Circus to Gabriela's last night... or this morning!

is wow what a surprise, still up and loving it... Boom, Boom, Boom, Boom...

is living fast, dying... never.

has been awake for 42 hours and is now mashed and wishing everyone a goodnight.

is so, so hung-over and is never drinking again!

wants to feel normal again.

is nursing an ordinary hangover.

is not drinking for the rest of her life and possibly the long weekend...

thinks oh dear, my head hurts!

is feeling the effects of Pisco Sours and Chilean Wine!

is burying her liver today, feel free to come and pay your last respects.

still feels a bit crap from yesterday! No cider for a while...

is totally blaming Jim for his hangover! And finds it hysterical that his cousin thought Jim was a girl!

is oh so very tired. Evil evil vino tinto.

got wasted last night and spent all my money... and actually shit the bloody bed!

is drunk enough to be bothered talking to you.

encourages everyone to witness the sickness.

is asking... has anyone got any spare eyebrows he can borrow?

should have said no to the Wobbly Wednesday - Never a good idea...

just got in at 7am from a pub crawl which ended at the British Luxury Club and is...

is trying to get over the Thursday night feeling before the Friday one kicks in!

tripped the fuck out earlier.

is hoping his liver is ready for another weekend.

is only getting back on his feet now after a weekend partying with the lads... Good craic, but it hurts!

is alive, just.

can't remember much of last night.

is resembling a lobster from an awesome weekend of lax, sun, beer, pirates, being floored and called a bloke!

doesn't think he will ever be the same again after this weekend...

just about remembers the weekend at Barnie's... unrivalled corpse comedy.

is still in shock that her friend went behind the DJ booth in Tokyo last night and turned the music off!

is shocked at the events of last night.

needs to stop wearing bikinis when he's pissed!

is very sore and needs to rethink the concept of trashy midweek partying.

is recovering from the session of a life time.

has a mouth as dry as an Iraqi's flip-flop, but had a grand old night!

is never drinking wine again!

thinks wine and vodka… baaaaad mix!

is so hung-over and trying to piece the night together! Blasted vodka! Another typical night at Side Bar!

is feeling rough after being on the buckets with Tom and Richard.

is ruined thanks to Adam Willy. Detoxification starts now!

had the most amazing weekend ever, can't remember any of it, but it must have been fun…!

is a dick… out on the lash… missed a flight… as Malin would say, "not good!"

is beyond hung-over and will not drink red wine for a while! Maybe even a week?

just had a bender in Boston and is waiting for a bus back to NYC.

had an awesome time last night, feeling it today though!

is in pain. Walked home bare foot last night and has huge blisters on the soles of my feet.

is remembering how drunk she really was after seeing the photos.

is fucked… and seriously needs to sort her dark circles out!

is giving up Sambucca for good!

lasted until 8am this morning! Twelve hours of madness, it hurts now, but what a wonderful weekend!

is still hung-over! No more red wine for me!

is sick as a small hospital… residents bar is always a good idea at the time :-(

is going to get back on it after one day being off the Goonage.

is just up… dazed and confused.

needs money for more drinking with Niall tonight… gonna pound my liver again!

is hung-over and semi-broke… damn you HQ!

regrets a lot of shit he did on the weekend but is really happy that Hampus did not run out of petrol while he was still in the car!

is feeling rather...

is really annoyed that the airline overbooked Emmett's flight and ruined tonight's plans.

is so proud of her little bro!

is in strange humour?

is excited about her weekend in Downings.

is soon on her way back to Stockholm and college hell! I'm feeling lonely!

is loving Manchester United 1—0 Liverpool.

is cream crackered like!

is the proud owner of a peacock wicker chair!

is sad she had to say goodbye to Rachael who is leaving for Hong Kong.

is missing Ben and Catherine and Simon and Daniel and Ghislain and Tony and Danny and Tiefi.

has never been happier!

is so pleased she ended up spending her Saturday with her favorite Irish man!

is exhausted after her day of filming in Bollywood (and very burnt).

is a nervous pervous!

is struggling and it's not even 9am.

is happier than ever.

is buzzing after jumping from 15,000ft over lake Taupo!

is love sick baby!

is feeling a lil under the weather!

is back home and it feels weird...!

is gutted at the death of her iPod and is preparing herself for its rebirth. Over 2,500 songs just gone! :(

is so happy not to be missing out on Forever Twisted.

is loving her cuddles :-)

is not happy that he can't get what he really wants...

is knackered and it's only Monday!

is chuffed someone handed in my camera to the police... thank god for good karma.

is shitting it about his skydive tomorrow...

is pissed off at the Marrone Boys no show.

is gutted, but is off to the Whitsunday's to cheer up!

is in an emotional state… fucking yes!

is missing Annette already.

is still in shock from yesterday! Just another day at HC.

is confused in Liverpool! Hmm?!

is in a bad mood!

is calm, as a don is supposed to be, Coso' Nostra…

is feeling like drinking.

is back in love with Richard Ashcroft.

is feeling super crap today.

is sick of it and hasn't even come close to finishing yet…

loves everyone, especially those ten girls.

is feeling good about life.

is in agony after burning her hand on the iron, and has been sent home to feel sorry for herself!

is in love—Paul Scholes do you wanna dance?

is depressed, tired and broke after Las Vegas.

is feeling super-bad. Not good.

is having a really sore throat and feels tired and weak.

is getting really stressed.

is feeling shithouse… and has another corker.

is glad it's the weekend, but completely fed up with one person in particular.

is feeling a little under the weather - no pun intended!

is excited, because if Gog is lost in Vegas and Jennie has gone looking, it means I've got peace and quiet!

is feeling just okay.

is sad to be leaving CSU and her friends in Colorado today, but excited to go on her American road trip.

is annoyed that the wish chips didn't work.

is nervous and anxious due to the wedding coming up soon… love you Sizar.

is disappointed in his own form last night.

is stoked she will not have to set the alarm for the morning.

is seething after being kept up all night by the guy who snores so loud my bed vibrated!

is glad that Murphy's Law saved the bullpit!

is feeling incredibly like Mick Jagger.

is powerless against fund raiser Freddie.

is desperately seeking Susan.

feels guilty about Charlotte's 4,500 words.

is worried that the shed he's having put up in the garden may end up as his permanent residence as it's costing more than the house!

is having to use matchsticks to keep her eyes open she is so tired!

is tired, stressed and in a very bad mood.

is rather sad to be leaving home sweet home, especially as the sun is shining but looking forward to Rome.

is disappointed he fell into Holly's food trap.

is disgusted at the house she viewed today… errghhh how can people live in such mess!

is getting nervous, but at least she gets to see her JEB tonight.

is pissed off she ain't got a tan yet!

is liking this American boy!

is ridiculously scared for tomorrow.

is a hungry, hungry… um… animal with "H" that's not a hippo…

is ill and low on karma :(Can't wait until Wednesday.

is pretty good thanks.

is stressed and may soon cry. Like Caroline and Katarina do…

is feeling alive again!

is sick like 100 dogs on the run in Victoria.

is having very mixed feelings about 12th June…

is sad that Sunday will be the end of an awesome pub!

is missing Canada… I want to go back :(

is not in a good mood about something.

is feeling the effects…

is pleased he has purchased Keane's new album.

is fed up with the smelly bus!

is wanting… after our conversation earlier, Gemma!

is glad Smithy's surgery went well, and is also pissing his pants that my inspirational speech got released!

is in agony, but buzzing!

is relieved to get out of that bloody cellar.

is worried her back may be broken… damn six inch heels.

is happy because her friend cheered her up… he knows who he is.

is feeling so ill!

is missing everyone that left me in this fuck-hole town!

has a funny feeling…

is glad to have some news from some French dudes!

is a lot happier… thank you.

feels bad enjoying tuna pasta without Barbara!

is feeling a little silly!

is not feeling so good now.

is very excited and proud that her parents just won Best Houseboat Builder in America!

is happy because we found our bird Jo, which is cool.

is feeling positively super!

feels like absolute shit… and wishes she could turn back time.

is tired but in strangely good humour?

is standardly bored by England.

is stressed and needs to make plans…

feels far better today… but what's the deal with drinking on antibiotics?

is bored and wants an old friend to message him so we can catch up.

feels as freaky as he wants to be…

is feeling very lucky to have a boyfriend who helps her so much whilst she's ill!

is deeply sorry for Samantha!

feels bad that she is crap at keeping in touch! But loves you all anyway!

is feeling a little better, thank God!

is not happy with the hacker.

feels like he is on holidays… four days off, you ripper!

is heartbroken… golden brown, from far away, never a frown…

is feeling pain after having a tooth pulled out!

is nervous, palms are sweaty, knees weak, arms are heavy, your mama is taking of his sweater already...

is feeling the PA magic.

is so excited, how quickly things change :-)

is impressed with herself for killing a really BIG spider.

is getting angry now.

is ambivalent about getting her stitches out. It's for the greater good but it's gonna hurt like a mother fucker.

is happy he got selected for the Queensland Young Auctioneers final!

is a bit cold this morning.

has mixed feelings about being Acting State Manager.

is feeling tiptop!

is sick, feeling rubbish and wanting to go home instead of being in work!

is feeling like a princess in beautiful Bali! Salam, Salam!

has a new default - so tired.

is GAY, GAY, GAY and feels FREE, FREE, FREE!

feels like an iceberg.

is feeling frustrated and it's giving her a sore head, but she will flip it, and the good times will return!

has just completed the Inca Trail and is not feeling too hot.

is happy... just happy...

is feeling very sleepy and depressed after the long road back from Arequipa.

is planning and is getting frustrated by it.

is feeling slightly guilty about shooting Brendan from point-blank range with a paintball gun.

is spending too much time on Facebook

is now jobless—the reason: wasting company time on Facebook.

is taking a break from Facebook for a few days.

is pissed off with Facebook as the fucking thing keeps crashing when I'm trying to upload my fucking pictures - sort it out Facebook!

is tidying up his Facebook because too many randoms have contacted him through clicking on engaged...

is tagging people in witness protection.

doesn't have enough brain cells left to think of a witty profile status.

is updating her status.

wants you to all join our group...

is getting sacked if she doesn't stop wasting company time on Facebook.

is weighing up whether to strangle Miller over his potentially border line inappropriate status update... this could make or break the friendship!

still hasn't finished her assignment and its due in tomorrow. Better get off Facebook then.

is thinking Facebook is the greatest, most evil thing the Devil has ever created.

's stupid sister added his dad to Facebook. Sorry if you find me untagging myself in photos, videos, etc...

is probably on Facebook right now... and probably not!?

is discovering why it's taken her so long to even begin to attempt to upload her very meagre photo collection to Facebook...

is on Facebook and therefore I am... how'd you like that Descartes.

thinks people should swear more in their status updates... F@&king aye Hollye Sutt...

is waiting for the T-whirl people to start tagging unattractive photos of her!

is currently featuring in thee worst photo album to be uploaded on Facebook. Ever!

has lost faith in laptops - PC or Mac.

is going to kick her shit Internet connection up the ass... and if she could throw it out the window...

now knows that five people read his status update.

is having withdrawal symptoms from not having the bloody Internet!

wonders how Donald is getting on... could there be a change in his "relationship status" soon?

is so fucking fucked off at Facebook. Someone please help before I smash up my computer.

finds it funny what you find out over Facebook!

is going to strangle the person who invented computer viruses.

thanks everyone for the birthday wall posts!

is getting back into MySpace.

aaarrrrgggghhhhh at Facebook!

is on a roll with bumper stickers.

's profile pic' is for the hottie on the right... love you Paula.

is fucking on a fucking splendour bullshit website.

says no need to crop this photo haha!

is not gonna dis you on the Internet, because my mamma taught me better then that!

is sick of having to make up a status every time he logs in.

wants bumper stickers... now!

is leaving Facebook for good. Please email me!

is wondering what percentage of Facebook status updates reference SATC this weekend.

cannot believe that Desmond has created a Facebook profile!

is angry his Facebook got hacked! Apologies to anyone who received a strange comment from me...

loves the nice things said over Facebook!

is tagging the spiral staircase that connects worlds.

would like all fans of The Walls to know that there is an official band Facebook page available now!

is having a .... HOUSE PARTY - Facebook event.

is Splendour Weekender... out of here until 26th October so Facebook me bitches.

can't think of anything reasonable to put as her status.

is thinking that Facebook is the Devil. The evilness is starting to transform!

is going to bash one out all over your Facebook!

says picture comments are usually seen by someone! DUUHHH!

is pissed the Internet doesn't work.

is stopping going on Facebook, it makes her too homesick.

has won a Facebook competition!

is not sending you those "legal bud" posts on your wall, it's a Facebook virus/bug/hack/thingy-m-gig.

is Facebooking when he should be sleeping!

will not be leaving his computer until next Monday night!

is going home to put her pictures up, be warned guys and girls! Hehe!

wants to break Facebook.

is loving Facebook chat, wish they could do this on Bebo, boooo.

has $16,671 in chips, on Owned.

is loving that her mum is now on Facebook! Welcome mother dear.

thinks her new profile picture sums her up… perfectly.

is finally uploading travel pic's!

is home :) and stealing next doors' wireless…

has finally put up her pic's of Laura, Hayley and Michelle's leaving party… so what if its three months late!

's all about his 1,110 fiends…

is hitting refresh like every ten seconds! We need to know where we are going…

should not be on Facebook.

is so happy that she got to talk to Ciaran on Facebook chat!

is saying sorry guys! Facebook wouldn't work for past 25 minutes so I missed my ending and accepting!

has new photos… comment please.

is so bored she Googled herself.

thanks Eileen for some awful pictures but some amazing memories!

is on Owned way too much…

has a new default, so comment on it bitches.

's Internet spat the dummy.

is miffed by Sam's negative status update. Sounds like a cry for help from a man mixed up in a bizarre love triangle.

hates the new Facebook. Put it back the way it was you dickheads!

is waiting for his picture's from last night so he can put them up.

says stop signing into my MSN!

has changed her profile picture for Mark - I love you!

is awfully confused at trying to speak to Inia and Ida at the same time on Facebook chat.

loves how many people have sent me the same bumper sticker :-)

is an idiot who thinks that by closing the browser window she is actually logging off her Facebook.

is mourning the loss of millions on Owned, but is kind of relieved to have got rid of it!

says sorry to the girls for the profile picture but it had to be done!

is so excited to be back on Facebook… *mwah*.

wonders why they would force a 'New Facebook' upon us? If it isn't broke don't fix it!

is crying as a result of Catherine's status!

just loves studying… hence being on Facebook.

is pumped up about his new privacy settings on Facebook, so only his 'friends' can see his stuff...
Goodbye stalkers!

is struggling for a status update

is happiest in A/C.

is sick of wearing trainers!

is knock, knock knocking on heavens door.

had a good day, thanks for asking.

is watching baby swallows annoy the magpie!

now has a fringe.

is listening to the new U2 album.

has been riding a scooter... well trying!

is going to the Zoo to see the baby elephants and giraffe with her mommy.

is rockin' the casbah.

was kung-fu fighting... that cunt was fast as lightning.

is with Sangita Mistry.

says sweet as bro!

is wondering who the fcuk Alice is?

is to you, to me, to you, to me...

is playing the bongo's... bum bada bum bada bum ching chang!

doesn't know what to say...

is ogling bling at Swarovski.

is a little pink!

doesn't have a sore tooth.

is old... totally cannot work new technology?!

is scared - a spider just landed on her head, eewh!

says PS. I love you.

is just getting down doing watta gotta do...

is somewhere over the rainbow.

wants you to say hello to his little friend... (wow... that sounded so much cleaner in my head!)

is a lover not a hater.

is ironing clothes no bigger than her hand.

is doing the electric boogaloo.

is walking around the Edmonton mall, and it is huge.

has come back to haunt you.

is having lunch on the King William Road today.

says; 'OMG the Hogan's have a monkey, it is so cute, the poor thing'.

is on level 32.

is right-handed trying not to use her right hand.

thought he saw someone he met in Cuba on TV today, and it would seem he did.

is in a New York state of mind.

is in his secret hiding place! Ssshhh.

wonders who came round and painted the Maccy D's olivey green?

is tripping the light fantastic.

is home from work and watching the world's smallest man, so funny.

is ironing! What's happened to me?!

is away, so is Callum and Bronac so message them lots and lots.

thinks who dares wins.

is singing along on his iPod.

is still on the grind, with a mill in the deal...

has finally had his back waxed!

is in so much pain :(

is the music man, he comes from far away, and he can play, oh yes he can!

... does my bum look big in this?

is alive with the sound of music, and needs a girlfriend...

thinks white men can't jump!

is off to see the one and only Richie Flip Flop tomorrow!

is disgusted that four bedroom houses are renting for 2,500 a month around his way!

has nothing constructive to add...

is on the computer next to her.

is all about the fridge at home!

is thinking there ain't no such thing as halfway crooks.

is the Terminator Four.

is shocked to learn that it takes eleven months for a pineapple to grow!

is wearing flip flops in the snow!

is hoping the wait proved worth it for you and it wasn't a waste of time.

is putting his bender shoes on...

sells sea shells by the sea shore.

is sequencing - what a dedicated coach!

is back in the motherland.

is wondering do I put my hair back to black or stay brown?

is so fresh and so clean.

is very grateful to Virgin for shepherding her wayward bag home safe and sound!

is in the company of two spiffing gentlemen.

is really hoping this van behaves this evening!

is like one of the Backstreetboys... it's not a good thing.

paved paradise and put up a parking lot.

is going to be paying for these four new tyres for the rest of her life!

is in desperate need of a haircut!

really, REALLY wants an iPod touch and wants to get another laptop as he is missing his so much!

is really struggling with Photoshop.

just took far too much time to decide what to write in this space and now realises that not only what she wrote was crap but that she will never get that hour back again!

is trying too hard

spits a sicker flow than the Rocky Horror Picture Show, just to let you bitches know we dope more than methadone.

is staring blankly into space whilst stroking his hirsute chin in the style of a baddie from Scooby Doo. Fo Shoo Be-hatch.

belongs in the Amazon with his forgotten tribe.

is wondering how tattoos went from being so cool to so, so, so uncool so quick. Any explanations—you at the back?

is talking da hardest… badman's on da block… all ma boys got same suit colour as batman…

"clouds appear free of care… and carefree drift away. But the carefree mind is not to be "found' - to find it, first stop looking around…" Wang An-shilh (1021-1086).

is clinging on to 99 red balloons—fly, damn you, fly!

says "if you drink a cup of tea and it feels rather hot… drop it like it's hot, drop it like it's hot".

is hanging tough, just like the New Kids!

thinks nothing cleanses like the champagne bath!

is Flanning flow, I just go, no huddle. Ya boys ain't balling, from the side, like Spike at the garden.

is iced out… see… I got an ice box where my heart used to be…

is no longer an IKEA virgin, I might even go visit that young Swedish lady again soon, she makes fantastic hotdogs!

is smoking a blunt!

sold his soul to the devil for his rugged good looks and unparalleled martial arts ability.

is contemplating a back, crack and sack number to complement his inability to grow a dashing beard.

says don't blame it on the sunshine, don't blame it on the moonlight, don't blame it on the good times!

is running out of time, and has got only 24 hours to save the world…

thinks man-flu must be worse than woman-flu. Except Scottish woman-flu, everyone knows that's as close to death as you can get.

is wondering where is all my ghetto bitches? Come back y'all.

eats pieces of shit like you for breakfast!

is of to climb Sydney Harbour Bridge… of course I'm not part of the organised bridge climbs… I don't need them… OK, maybe I do just a lil bit!

thinks Cram McRam is superbad… as in good.

wouldn't mind taking her top down like a play boy bunny...

is recovering from an "electric" night out! See what I did there? Bad puns all round!

says OK, so it's been seven hours since she swallowed a pip, and still no tree!

is smokin' the finest of the Cali green, hit the bong [reload].

has got big things popping and little things stopping, you could walk up in my crib and go mall shopping...

is ghost, like Swayze.

's hobbies include wearing Blundstones to Uni, drinking wine in public and shameless self promotion.

is cheap tickets for Billy Elliott: $45, Drinks: $10, Blagging into the Royal Box: Priceless.

and still I see no changes, misplaced hate makes disgrace for races, we're under, I wonder what it takes to make this one better place, let's erase the wasted.

is Macking that!

says war on decks, yeye. War on mics. I'll teach your girlfriend bout oral sex, yeye, that's what I like, yeye, that's what I'm like, I'm in the spotlight!

is hungry. What shall he have for dinner, Bats heads or Maggots?

spent over twelve hours at work again! I get paid well but what price is there on free time especially when you have got a whirlpool on your rooftop terrace.

is doing that thing they get paid to do

has been working all day and is on all day tomorrow, but wondering whether to go out and get leathered for the eight hours in between?

is in a suit at a desk in an office... EEEKK!

is@work.co.uk/tired.

is now moving furniture for a grand a week.

is off to work... even though she's feeling slightly rough! A bottle of champagne might help?!

is glad she found a job in Peru she actually likes =)

so does not have the patience required to teach six year olds!

is a world champion time waster!

has a job... YES A JOB... no-one fall on the floor!

is at work. Surprise, Surprise!

is working at a wedding tonight, Oh lala...

has completed about a million little jobs today :)

is strawberry picking south of Christchurch... one for you, two for me... nice.

is sick of copying and pasting...

is getting the black lung from working in this shit hole, but it's worth it for the adventure that awaits!

is not happy to be working on a Sunday...

is pleased but slightly confused that she received a present for Secretary's Day today. She is not a secretary!

is back to blasted work again, but would rather go the beach :-(

is bored today... and very tired from the 21 hour work weekend she just had...

starts a new job today. Will this one last more than four shifts?

is not in the humour for work today.

is a tagging machine!

survived her first day at work!

is now officially a cleaner / bus driver in Cairns and looks fucking hot in his apron.

is taking photos all week and being given money for it!

has worked 28 hours in two days! That is not what I call a holiday!

is avoiding all the work she should be doing.

is off to work for the second time today.

was playing GTA4... that's right GTA4! And all while I was at work today.

is beginning to realise they don't call it busy season for no reason!

is happy with his new job as a fork lift driver... someone actually trusts me with a fork lift!

is just about to knock off and have a beer.

is loving Mondays in work... WTF has happened to me?

needs bar staff members available for both days and nights. Anyone know people that may be interested?

is going it alone and I am going to do it my way...

is bored as work has been very slow today.

has just got an account manager job for an Ad agency!

is now sitting between Joakim and Andreas at work - you lucky fellows!

is a night manager in his new job, how good is that? And we played the funniest game of bingo last night!

spent more time at work than at home this weekend!

is not looking forward to her 15 hours of working tomorrow and Thursday!

is contemplating becoming a professional folder organiser.

is at work and hates it.

knows way too much about CH and can't wait to share on Monday!

is sorting out music for work.

has started back at work for the first time in three months! Not happy!

is not happy that she has to work tonight - it's been a long week!

got a part time job until I know what I want to do.

is gonna be working with the moose-fucker John 'hound dog' Quinn for the next month.

is working hard... I think not!

is desperately looking for more labourers, if you're looking for work or know a guy who is, get onto me ASAP. Soft cocks need not apply.

is working at the dental hospital tomorrow... can't wait.

is no longer unemployed.

has enjoyed his day off, now he's looking forward to Friday when he has another day off.

is sleeping at work again.

can't believe I made it through the whole day at work today feeling like total dog shit!

is working in a restaurant with a cool chef, a funny man.

is doing double shifts in the restaurant, and loves it.

is filing... someone shot me please.

enjoys working at the children's dental department at the hospital and can't wait for Monday morning.

is very busy at work today, like a bumble bee!

is trying to get this new tip-ex pen thingy to work.

handed his notice in today.

is hungover but working really hard at Riverdance.

has had one of the most hectic Tuesdays ever, but you just got to love this business.

is working from home tomorrow... so you know what that means...

is employed... so let's buy new suits!

stocktake, stocktake, stocktake... la la la la la la la.

is not looking forward to the ten hour shift tonight. Should be a good night though.

is back in the world of employment and is finding it surprisingly enjoyable. God knows I won't be saying that at the end of this week!

is so looking forward to enjoying her first day off work in five weeks!

is a professional fruit picker!

has had enough of work and wants 'to gome'.

is leaving the office at 22.54... loser!

has been working hard and can't wait to sleep!

is sore from working too hard... anyone do good massages?

just finished a 14.5 hour day and feels like I can take on a bit more of what life has to throw at me.

is '"away on business" in Cairns! Sun, bikinis, koalas and kangaroo's! What a trip!

is wanting a new job... NOW!

is enjoying her late start this morning. She loves Mondays!

has a very busy day ahead.

is now in charge of the business for the week—got some long days coming up.

has had quite enough of this 'work' malarkey for one week.

is hoping the drunken scary guy stalking her at work goes away soon!

is sorry he missed Maliya's last day at work, but was touched by her card.

is totally wiped out tonight... all this work is slowly catching up with him!

can't be arsed to go back to work tomorrow.

is so tired it is not funny and is working AGAIN tonight followed by tomorrow daytime AGAIN :-(

is having a relaxed Friday afternoon in work.

is looking forward to the night shift, peace and quiet!

is marking assignments all day! Bring on Rory's BBQ tomorrow!

has got a job that pays 24 dollars an hour and as many hours as I want!

is looking forward to tapas and sangria at three, courtesy of work! Got to love work... sometimes!

is not best pleased about his 13 hour shift yesterday!

is sick of speaking to stupid and stinky people at work! But what can you do, it's my job!

is actually working at this time of night... WTF!

has blood down his top. Gonna have to get used to these Aussie staff meetings...

is sick to death of working with incompetent people!

had a great time camping but is now off to work on a public holiday. Yet another 14 hour day!

is the Stocktaking King... no... not really... actually not at all!

is asking: "Why the hell cant people do their jobs right?"

went home for six hours last night then came back to the office :-(

is plum tuckered from photo shooting ALL day!

doesn't mind this fruit picking lark, it's actually alright like!

is happy because the photo-shoot was great and she's really satisfied with the result. Great pictures and great cooperation!

is not happy about getting up at 5:30am every morning to go to work - not good.

is working and shit!

should not be at work, she should be...

is happy in his hoodie on a Friday - I don't care if I'm working, that's just were it's at.

is really enjoying my new job. Cool people to work with.

had a busy first day back at work.

is tired from last night but is made up that he actually made it in to work quite fresh!

had the most unproductive day at work ever... why can't people keep appointments!

is officially working seven day weeks at Big Brother!

is wondering if everyone had a good long weekend? He worked every fucking night...

is home from work... whey funny night though :)

got the day off work due to lack of trousers.

is pissed she can't get time off work to watch Olivier do his thing :(

woke up at 4am this morning to deliver newspapers with Ross! The world has certainly gone topsy turvy.

is still waiting for his new fucking website and starting to get the severe hump!

is on night shift, yay! (extreme sarcasm).

is thinking of taking up an offer to work in Dubai for nine months. Sounds interesting!

is at work and looking forward to finishing up!

is shackled to her desk right now but shall be breaking free very shortly to give Ninoska a slightly hysterical and probably gin-soaked welcome back to Paris!

is at work and is very bored as she has nothing to do.

is sick and tired of the Crazy Big Sale and wants a day off.

does not agree with that behaviour in the workplace.

is not wanting to go to work as she is loving her new bed :)

is amped to be going away this week. Even if it is for work.

has been picking tomatoes and sweet potatoes for the last two days. Literally a pain in the back!

is nailing a big deal at work today...

is not being productive enough!

has a massive new whiteboard in the office, love it! Let the creativity flow!

is working hard at her new job, but dreaming of traveling.

has just finished fruit picking woo woo! Can't wait to go on my holiday now and wear my Wellingtons.

is supposed to be out of the office two hours ago... Grrr! But at least it's Friday and I've finally found a reason to thank the Queen of England!

is out of the country

talk Thai. Johanna talk Thai real good!

is letting everyone know she has arrived safely in Tonga, and that her Peru number no longer works!

is Amsterdamaged.

is freezing in Hanoi—It's seriously cold!

is bruising his way around Korea with his 38 inch guns... where?

is looking forward to tubing down the Mekong!

is worried that Tibet is covered in snow and averaging about -18 degrees when he gets there in two weeks!

is heading up to Sa Pa tonight for a couple of days trekking. It's about to get even colder.

is living the dream in New Zealand and loving all the crazy things she's done since arriving!

is amazed in Zion, NM because it feels like Mexico.

is loving Fiji and looking forward to starting my advanced diving course tomorrow! 30 meters baby!

is in Lanta, and the sun is out!

is in Hoi An, Vietnam, about to go crazy in the tailor shops - well a girl can never have too many dresses!

is away in the Holy Land.

is in Rotorua and looking forward to the Maori culture evening.

is about to get a night train to Chang Mia... were I'm gonna be knocked out with my cock out!

is in transit to Myanmar, land of little Internet!

is on her way to Kuala Lumpur.

is rounding up the troops for St Patrick's day in La Paz!

is back in a land of good roads, polite people, courteous drivers, mandatory headscarves and women haters. Goodbye Pakistan, hello Iran.

is in sunny Waiheke and can hear the vineyards calling her name.

is in Bangkok raiding the markets.

is looking forward to home cooked food after eating sushi most of the past three months.

is going to the big hole today, AKA the Grand Canyon.

is off to the South Island to find some Hobbit's.

is drinking Riesling in the Rhine valley... Whoop whoop!

is in Ireland :-) The land of good Guinness, good greens and good girls...

is simply in Taos.

is in Koh Samui, Thailand, and is off to see a huge rock hard penis.

is living the dream in New Zealand.

is in Greymouth. Grey by name, grey by nature.

is desperate to squeeze a bit more bikini time out of Oz.

is in Prungioweiolskjslkjslöwysoireofopkfkofkfölömchydtgwbenffppoesdfäösdeahasqwatrtröarnistan

is amazed by Auckland... its freezing, rainy, full of Paddy's... yet surprisingly, he wants to stay!

is home soon... but not for long!

is sorry to tell everyone in the UK that due to foreseen circumstances he is not returning to London and is indeed moving to Barcelona!

is in Tel Aviv and heading to Haifa tomorrow. Israel is wicked!

is loving Serbia and Slovenia, but OMG Macca's here still using Styrofoam containers!

is chewing this horrible juicy fruit flavoured toothpaste from Iraq. WTF?

is in Buenos Aires, Argentina! Bring it on! This place is crazy.

is in Luang Prabang preparing herself for two weeks in the middle of nowhere in Northern Laos.

is in Franz Josef and has just walked over the Glacier!

esta en Paraguay!

is never going to experience an earthquake at this rate. Come on Australia!

is in non-English-speaking land.

is still laughing at bad Iranian reversing, and still shocked it cost less that seven quid to fill the bus here!

is hoping her nephew has a nice Christening tomorrow and I'm sorry I'm not able to attend but misses everyone all the time! Only six months until I return... and not for babysitting, haha.

is an insomniac in beautiful Teaneck, NJ.

crossed the biospheres today, goodbye Asia, hello Istanbul and civilisation!

is en route to Portugal.

is back in Sydney after an Ozbus style marathon journey involving an eight hour diversion to Brisbane!

is feeling the heat in Kuala Lumpur!

is about to head off for a Lao massage and herbal sauna and will be rehydrating herself with nice cocktails.

is playing with crocodiles in Darwin.

is looking forward to salsa dancing her way through the next six weeks!

is now in Calcutta, and got a new phone so please email your numbers.

is on 'Struggle Street' in Roma.

is thinking how absolutely beautiful it is here in Northern Ireland.

is feeling the burn in Mexicooo.

is missing New Zealand fucking big time, but thinks Alcudia is not a bad trade off!

is whale watching in Kaikoura.

has just spent three hours in a British pub right in the heart of Cusco... got to love cheesy chips!

is in Paradise. It's an island just off the Caribbean!

is in a town called Baños, yes it's Spanish for toilet and I spent a bit of time in there also...

is in Tulum. Staying in a little hut on the beach.

is on his way back to Strabangladesh, after a wicked time in Kathmandu.

is off to the Tanami Desert!

is in beautiful Lake Tekapo... well not actually in the lake, in the village next to it!

has been cruising around a Caribbean island in a golf buggy all day.

is sweating it out in Flores.

is in El Tunco, El Salvador looking at black sand and white water.

is in chilly Chile.

is in Guatemala. Were her phone is driving her insane.

just swam with around 40 dolphins in Kaikoura treaty... and Declan!

is in Italian Switzerland somewhere?

is in Honduras and loves Headman Allas.

is ready for one last night in Lisboa then back to the US.

is in Vegas and he's in profit.

is on an island just off Honduras, with the s.l.o.w.e.s.t. and most expensive Internet ever.

only has one week left in Mexico :(

is in the driest desert on Earth (but brought an umbrella, just in case)!

can't believe how cold it is again in Kyiv!

is in the Dominican... come out sunshine... we know you want to play!

says bye bye to Cambodia and hello to Vietnam!

is off to Tiberius this evening and then to Jerusalem in a couple days.

has survived the Atacama desert!

is in Argentina and gutted the ski lifts are closed!

is in LA missing the moustache gang!

knows what San Fran-of-fucking-cisco can do to your ass, six hours going up, up, up and a little down!

is back in Auckland... Tahiti gets closer and closer...

is leaving Utila. Next stop Copan.

is in Puerto Madryn and gonna check out some whales tomorrow.

is safely in Panama city in Florida and flying back to London tomorrow, hopefully not via Zimbabwe.

is in Antigua preparing to face the volcano.

has been on a bus tour of La Paz... interesting... NOT!

is in humid Singapore =)

is finally in Tahiti... what an expensive jungle!

has extended her time away and is not coming home yet!

is loving Switzerland, cheese, annoying Russian kids and all!

is in arequiparequiperaquipera.

is in Vang Vieng northern Laos where she has added to her cuts, scrapes and bruises with just a tad of rock climbing today.

is trying to rub it in

is either sailing, white-water rafting, driving 4X4s, oxygen assisted skydiving, on safari, in rain forest, scuba diving, snorkelling, partying or sleeping.

is waiting on the weather to cool down, so I can go to the beach.

is back from a lovely weekend in the Blue Mountains and is already missing her five star luxuries.

is going to see The Prodigy tonight!

is tantastic!

is loving working by the beach this week :-) Sun!

is surfing six foot rollers boiiiieeee!

is happy with her packages from home! Lots of more clothes for Miss Jeavons!

loves having her best friend as a hairdresser.

is at the beach having a bit of R&R after a busy weekend in Saigon, Vietnam.

is still pumping with adrenaline from his 60 seconds freefall skydive.

is doing New Zealand's highest bungee soon. Scared? Yes.

has just kayaked the entire ocean...

is letting everyone know her Bali number so I don't miss you too much, its +6271XXXXXXXXXX.

is looking forward to modelling for Wimbledon Fashion Week this summer.

found where all the hot Brits hang out - IBIZA baby! Good times!

is going to get his oxygen mask on, get 15,000ft up in the sky... locate his testicles... then jump out!

has been sleeping on the beach today.

is celebrating! I was tonight crowned poker king.

has just arrived in Queenstown and can't wait to party!

is now an advanced diver and is feeling like shit after the celebration last night.

has just booked flights from Melbourne to Cairns - the smell of the East Coast adventure is in the air!

is not well at all but still managed to chill in a spa today.

is loving Sydney. It's February and he's going to the beach now :-)

has REM tickets, hurray - only five months to wait!

is going to the water park, the open air cinema, two beaches and the A League Football Final. And maybe out for a beer or two - Not a bad weekend if I do say so!

is trying to find his manhood and book a skydive!

is diving with Nemo. (Sinking like a damn rock!).

is an adrenaline junky!

has just thrown herself off a cliff and swung over a canyon!

is stoked and has the best girlfriend in the world.

is so happy, because he jumped 134 meters in a bungee yesterday!

can't believe she's about to drive a 4x4 and spend two nights camping!

is a bird or maybe a plane... actually no she's... just jumped from a plane!

is a certified diver! Have we got tickets or what! HAHA we can go diving naked.

has got a busy few weeks to finish Australia!

is sunbathing and working... at the same time.

is looking forward to seeing The Phantom of the Opera tonight!

is OMG I am loving Surfers Paradise! I want to live on the beach forever!

can't wait to pick up her Wicked Camper with Dale, Pete, Adam and Carl! Wooo road trip!

is asking does anyone want to come to Portugal with her tomorrow?

is saying: 'Egypt here we come'! Whoop whoop!

has got tickets for Simian tomorrow night for me, Hanna and Milly, guys and babes.

is off to France next Saturday to see her Daddy! Bonjour!

has just snorkelled the Great Barrier Reef! How many of you lot can say that!

loved white water rafting in the jungle, but hated the fucking spiders!

is going scuba diving today in Thailand!

trekked the great wall of china... what an experience!

is most definitely peeing my pants over the sea from 14,000 feet up!

is tired and bruised after her extreme white water rafting, but is now a pro!

is going to see Carl Barron tonight.

is gloriously sunburnt driving around on her moped in Macedonia.

loved swimming with the tropical fishies on the reef.

is thinking oh my god, how different is Bangkok to Pattaya? He's going to have some good times here!

passed her open water baby.

is heading south to snorkel on the Red Sea reef tomorrow.

is having a great time in Melbourne.

is loving her new house. It's sooo nice, new and cosy!

is caving, abseiling, rock climbing, black water rafting and getting cold - all in one day.

is in Calafate checking out the world's biggest glacier.

is going on a four seater plane to do loop-the-loops and other crazy stuff in the sky! Yeha!

is attempting to get a sun tan in beautiful Santorini.

is recovering from a weekend at the beach, it's a hard life!

is on the beach...

surfed with the dolphins today, and it was the best feeling ever.

has survived the Inca Trail!

is back from Turkey and several shades darker...

is cruising in his Toyota Previa Deluxe, in Los Angeles, California, USA.

is loving her hotel suite in Korea that the airline are paying for :-) I've a huge TV, couch, PC, minibar, DVD player, Jacuzzi tub and one of those toilets that wash you!

is so unbelievably unprepared to climb the volcano tomorrow.

just came back from Rome...

is in Radelaide after a wicked trip through the outback and is going wine tasting tomorrow.

is all dived out.

has one more day in New Zealand, then off to Fiji!

is fucking loving Turkey!

is in San Salvador, partying with the second runner up in the Miss El Salvador beauty pageant.

finally has a stunning house...!

is surfing Verde Seven.

is after booking a holiday from her holiday... Fiji baby, wha ha ha!

is in Dubrovnik and ready to chill on a boat.

is back from Alicante and is getting ready for a big P.A.R.T.Y in Malia with the girls :-)

is at the coolest place on earth...

got to go Jet-boating for free today... yeeaahh!

is in Melbourne and is now going to party for the next ten days before he leaves Oz for the Thailand.

is going to watch killer whales smash sea lions today.

got the last two tickets to Michael Buble for tonight and she can't wait!

is loving the holiday life... bring on the binge drinking!

is in the bar! Ibiza is hot!

is heading up to Bariloche to hit some mad skiing action.

is in Cusco for Machu Piccu on Monday.

is hot, hot, hot in Ibiza with some lovely people... kiss my arse London!

is a huge sports nut

has been entered into a snooker competition after a fluke game... oh dear, I'm gonna fail miserably!

is preparing for his tennis match!

is thinking he might get a little wet today at the Footie...

is a European Gold Medalist, Madrid '08.

is very happy with his six-a-side-team!

is needing to know who number 28 in the Sydney Swans is... any fans please help me out!

is resting after an intense hockey game!

is taking a gun to the old boys match.

is so looking forward to Go-karting on Thursday!

is hoping the rain and hail stays away so that Gary can make it two in a row!

is in a horrible mood after the game!

is well excited about going to her first live AFL game, come on the Swans!

is never tipping the Crusaders again... How did they lose? The mind boggles!

wants to come home and fight on this show in the MEN... I miss getting in the ring so much.

is wondering how a pretty harmless Shiv tackle ended up like this.

is just saying 'good on ya boys for wining the cup. Proud of you all...'

fancies a ball game! Anyone for golf?

is winning in the Conflictus Maximus trophy...

is urging people to sponsor him for the London Triathlon. See profile page and click on Just Giving.

is off to kick 40 goals against Adelaide Uni.

is officially rooting FOR the Spurs - he knows it's weird - But Kobe is NOT MVP!

is annoyed she did so shite in her Footie tips this week :(

has had another horrendous play-off final weekend!

is thinking the Eagles are back after Saturday night's awesome win!

is pumped that punter is back in form.

is doing research and knows now who he fancies for the derby.

is sitting, waiting, and wishing he didn't go for that spoil midway through the fourth quarter.

is going to quit Footie... it's raining.

is thinking tequila, table football and a nap... beautiful.

is fired up about Collingwood's 85 point thrashing of Geelong. Go the Pies.

is shouting common the Royals!

is pretty bad at chess!

is watching game six of Hornets v Spurs, even though she knows the result!

met some of the F1 teams at work tonight!

is less than stoked about the Bulls result at the weekend.

is mega stoked that the Coasters got over the Crows. Bloody good on you Wirra.

is singing Up the Dale, Up the Dale, Up the Dale!

is playing in a hockey tournament in the Netherlands this weekend.

can't wait to stay undefeated tomorrow.

is getting ready for the Sharks game! Can't wait!

is about to be beat 4 - 0 in Scrabulous... the shame. He will beat someone at Scrabulous someday!

is home from his epic fishing adventure!

is saying 'sucked in' to all you Bombers fans. A win's a win.

is off for a surf!

is hoping that Shep's won after being 5 - 4 up in injury time? If not he only has himself to blame for conceding so many goals.

is saying 'Go Fuck yourself San Diego'!

is envious of the Mo on the goal umpire at the Sharks game!

is dumbfounded! What is with the 49er's last quarters?

has to go to bloody training, and will be sober all weekend.

is back into the netball vibe...

is not very happy with the Tigers second half.

says: 'Go on the Celtics', and loving Celtics 2 - 0. I feel another Celtics Championship!

is getting ready for Polo.

is pissed off, as he's trying to watch the Footie, but a stupid wasp is tormenting him!

isn't sure whether to back England in the Cricket or not.

is being forced to watch the Footie—AGAIN!

partied with the Sydney Swans last night! Oh my good god! So exciting.

is aching after a long weekend of judo in Holland!

is done in. Boxing is a killer!

is watching the Tigers instead of being on the daily grind...

is pretty sure someone owes him dinner, thank you Carlton!

thanks Adam and Alesha for keeping me updated with the Hawks emphatic win.

is still laughing at Redmond's winning speech.

wants everyone to look for the Kenny Flacentino banner at the Footie tonight!

is proud of the Tyrone! Unlucky Kerry!

is very sore from Wrestling.

won 200 Baht at Thai Boxing last night... How much is that?! About $6... the Milky Bars are on me!

is going skiing and drinking, bad combination, but let's go Bynski!

is hoping the Crows can beat the Hawks.

is happy its Wobbly Wednesday... indoor hop scotch! This is war! I will have victory!

is counting down the days until Gutman is at a NAFC game.

prefers it when teams don't cheat...

is glad she gave up three hours of study to see Essendon kick Carlton's arse!

went out surfing today and seen a fin ten meters away from Him. He thought it was a shark so he shit himself, but it was just a dolphin! Haha!

is in need of a win!

is heading to the Gabba to watch the Crows get eaten by the mighty Lions... ROOAARR.

is getting up to watch Tiger dominate the play offs!

is embarrassed over his performance at Echunga yesterday... wonder if my putter is still stuck on the seventh fairway snapped in two!

is rooting for the Lakers.

is happy to be awarded Players Player of the Season.

says bring on the (pussy) Cats.

is looking forward to Ascot and hoping for another 25/1 long shot win like last year.

is getting pumped for Footie.

is frothin' on the Celtics of Boston's game six demolition of the Lakers of Los Angeles.

is staggered at the Rookies form.

needs her immune system to kick in before the netball today and going out tonight!

is recovering from a brilliant day at Ascot and still has cash in his wallet—result!

has a big game today, and a big night tonight.

is playing Squash today for the first time in six weeks with only 20 minutes training under his belt.

is off to Wimbledon tomorrow.

is in Melbourne and went to watch the 'Roos today! I now think Hawthorn have the most feral supporters!

is a huge football nut

is loving Dirk Kuyt right now! But doesn't know how to feel about Riise… Stupid Fucker!

is thinking Arsenal are going to bottle it!

was feeling a little under the weather, but feels better now watching the THFC game… come on Spurs!

is gonna be livin' la vida loco if United win tonight!

is thinking if United win tonight, its Moscow on the 21st.

is nervous about playing St. Pats.

can ping a long ball with the best of them. Gazza, Gerrard and Cummings. England's finest!

is finally a Premiership winning indoor soccer player.

is a Liverpool / Chelsea fan for the final… f**k Ferguson… messy alcoholic!

is thinking where have all the Zinedine's gone?

believes that Liverpool can do Chelsea tomorrow!

is signing "Steve Gerard, Gerard, he kisses the badge on his chest, then hands in a transfer request…"

is laughing at the crying Scousers… love it…

is thinking, it's not a trick is it, English football?

is over the moon! Bring on Moscow! Boomshakalaka!

is standing on his sofa screaming at the top of his voice "… there will be thousands of Reds, we will be pissed of our heads, cos United are going to Moscow. Ya Nigh Ted, Ya Nigh Ted, Ya Nigh Ted"

is a melon. Play up Pompey.

reckons as much as he hates Cardiff, he still wants them to win the FA cup.

is preparing for the trip to Wembley with Leeds next weekend!

is singing "we love you Bolton" and is happy the league title was won at Wigan, and stays in the North!

knows that the double is on!

is laughing at the Chelsea Rentboys, and how they will win nothing this season!

is loving the fact Fulham will be playing top flight football again next season, cos that's just how we roll.

is shouting come on Carlisle!

is not being nosey or anything but does anyone know anyone who has ever seen the Scousers win the league? Seriously, someone must know somebody who has!

is thinking Mathieu Flamini is a cunt.

is gonna keep believing Leeds can do it. Thursday is our biggest day for a long time, come on Leeds!

is home early from work watching the Champions League with the boys! Let's get STEAMING!

is not a Sunderland fan anymore… I just lost a bet.

is pleased he queued for over an hour for the new kit… COYS.

is singing "We shall not, we shall not be moved" and "We are staying up, we are staying up."

is next stop, Moscow! Come on you reds!

is saying heads up Chelsea, we still got Moscow.

still salutes the best team in the world… Celtic.

is off to the Lane to see Liverpool kick Spurs' arse. Sy get your readies ready!

can't wait until Sunday, Wembley here we come, Leeds, Leeds, Leeds!

is hoping Chelsea kick Man United's arse!

is praying for a Chelsea win tonight…

is cheering, Com'on Man United! Lets dick on them again!

is backing the South for one night only, although Liverpool should be in the final!

is nervous and counting down the minutes… Com'on Reds. COM'ON REDS!

is preparing for Everton Vs MLS Part II, this time live on TV, watch out for the overhead kick.

is librarying it up before UEFA Cup!

is thinking Rangers fans are scum! Go home!

is stoked that the Wanderers have survived! Do I hear a championship next year? Or is that too soon…?

is singing we all follow the Arsenal.

loves it. The best team in Europe again, United forever!

is saying, Terry you got what you deserved.

hates those Manc cunts.

is singing "lets all laugh at Terry, lets all laugh at Terry…"

still fucking hates Man United! I quite like Wellington though, it's cool!

is thinking John Terry had the world at his feet! Haha! What a game!

is saying they think it's all over… it is now!

is lost for words. We fucked it up again. I also can't understand why the moronic Arsenal fans I know are getting so excited when they have won fuck all… AGAIN!

is going to Wembley on Sunday to watch Leeds… no glory supporters there!

is still laughing at how cocky Terry was as he walked up to take the Penalty, dreeeaaaming of getting the England armband… what happened next is pure comedy!

has a ticket for Australia v Ghana tomorrow… any takers…?

is pressing hard for Raul to be re-instated to the Spanish national team.

says Sir Alex will not be denied.

is pissed off with the fact that the arse of Leeds United always falls out when the get to a sodding final!

is gutted Chelsea lost!

hates soccer at the moment…

is Everton FC until I die. Go on you Toffee's.

went to the football, and the weather was shit. Not impressed that no one else from security turned up.

is angry and disappointed with Leeds United.

had an amazing day at Wembley and is a proud fan of Rochdale.

is excited about going to see Flamengo play!

is angry that Theo Walcott's weak right foot cost him $35.

needs to stop watching football and go and look at tracing…

is praying that Ronaldo follows up on his word and fucks off to Spain… Who is laughing now United?

can't believe the Socceroos lost.

is watching Euro 2008 with a feeling of bitterness towards McClown for making this summer so boring.

is real proud of the role model like performance he gave in goal today :)

just watched River win the title! Vamos River Plate—Champions!

is hoping Poland kicks ze Germans asses!

is watching BBC3… and is very smug at getting every Euro result right so far, show me the money Ladbrokes.

is in the European Cup fever :-)

is watching the Euro's and thinking… WHY? Cheers McClaren!

is giving a bleary-eyed salute to Valencia's finest… David Villa!

is saying bring on Scolari.

is thriving on all of this football… mind you the French are bloody woeful!

has tickets to watch Austria get their football dreams destroyed by Poland. 'GO POLSKA.'

is wishing he was Spanish, go on the Red Fury!

is happy Austria and Polska tied, just means the German vs. Austria game will be even better.

is sulking… If you hate the Spanish stand up!

is wondering what club he should join before the transfer window closes… so many choices, so little time!

is hoping Spain clean up those dirty Russians tonight.

does not want to but has asked for a transfer to change clubs today… He just wants to play in the first team!

is enjoying a beer while watching the Euro's, go on Holland!

is happy that Croatia stole in for the win at the last minute.

is stoked that both the Netherlands and Italy won last night!

is hoping the Swedes get up, just to piss off Drago for loving the Russians!

thinks Lampard to Inter? Is this the worst off-season ever?

is calling to arms the Basque ETA… target, Russia v Holland.

does not know why he just went mental about the Turkish goal!

is a proud Manchester United fan. Champions of England. Kings of Europe. 6 Feb 1958, Duncan, Harry, et al R.I.P.

is offering an insight... I think

believes it is better to be a didgeridoo than a didgeridont.

is letting you know that it is the passion that is in a kiss that gives to you its sweetness; it is the affection in a kiss that sanctifies it.

's horoscope for today says - living a good life is the best revenge!

has decided the most selfish thing to do is to blame selfishness on someone less selfish in an attempt to decrease the degree of selfishness in the first instance!

is giving you some advice: if you don't, don't.

thinks you're showing someone you've moved on by living your life.

is telling you to follow your bliss!

admits that the language of friendship is not words but meanings.

is saying get off your knees Eleanor, you don't see me on them do you! You're better than this!

agrees that it's true, life will smile for you.

...not a speck of light is showing, so the danger must be growing, are the fires of hell a-glowing, is the grisly reaper mowing...?

says good, better, best, never let it rest, until your good is better and your better is best.

is "the east, and Juliet is the sun."

thinks love is the fountain of life-giving water. No one and no thing can live without love.

is thinking that life is too short to be worrying about pissing God off!

admits that it is what it is, nothing more, nothing less.

loves the Chinese proverb 'A child's life is like a piece of paper on which every passer-by leaves a mark.'

is letting you know that I can read you like a book.

believes that not everyone is perfect, and we are bound to make mistakes... but the meanings are there...

is just trying to let you know that you should get the f**k out when you can!

agrees "good guys fuck you over, bad guys fuck you over and the rest don't know how to fuck you at all."

is saying... listen close to what you see.

thinks you never really understand a person until you consider things from his point of view.

is thinking that when life gets tough, give the fuck up!

doesn't agree with the fact that each person's nipples are nine inches apart. Let's prove them wrong girls.

is thinking that if you love me, you won't let me go.

is letting you all know I will follow my path no matter how often I loose my way.

remembers the old truth, that if you don't respect your own Armed Forces, you will fairly soon find that you have to respect someone else's.

is letting you know that I can read you like a book.

knows that this is our time. Our time to turn the page on the policies of the past and bring new energy and new ideas to the challenges we face.

is thinking beauty goes deeper than just the outside appearance.

thinks that Laurence Fennemore really should have a good look at himself…

is nice feeling important but believes it's more important to be nice.

thinks just because someone seems nice, doesn't mean you can trust them.

realised that life sometimes hits you right in the face!

says: 'if you can't convince them, confuse them'.

… were you born to resist or be abused…? I swear I'll never give in, I refuse!

wonders why if alcohol fixes all the problems of the world, don't they sit in the Whitehouse and get smashed… Oh hang on maybe that's why America is so fucked right about now.

is only at this late stage starting to understand that silence is the secret to success.

says: 'I learned to walk as a baby and I haven't had a lesson since'.

is telling A-town to watch out for their pockets.

is telling you to have a break, have a shit-kat.

is wondering why you look at the speck of sawdust in somebody's eye, yet pay no attention to the plank in your own.

is wishing things were different

wonders why are you getting worse Philipp? Please get better, knock me out and give me some abuse! You are my lover and you are always there when I need you. I don't know what to do!

is not leaving her room with this fat lip!

my lover, Joffy, you are my world, I love you so much. Please come back to me… I need you.

is officially on holidays, yet officially has tonsillitis!

cannot believe how much the UK has gone down the pan in just a year, it sucks to be English and live in the UK - tell me otherwise if you can!

is really hating Murphy and his laws.

is pissed off people keep leaving me voice messages and just hanging up. Annoying!

thinks you're slack.

is apologising for being distant, just wants and needs Mark back!

doesn't want to leave NYC...

is back home in London and needs some friends to keep him sane.

wants to go travelling again... forever!

is shocked by how much has already changed at home. I've only been gone nine months, slow down people, what is the big rush?

loves love her way... sigh.

is saying everyone could you please stop talking shit to my Ex. We are over, so let it be. And Katrina, find your life again please, because I don't want to see you ruined.

guesses he now knows who his real crew is...

is losing her arm again...

can't believe the gap year ends tomorrow.

is wondering... will he ever learn?!

wants a brand new house from an episode of MTV Cribs, with a bathroom I can play baseball in and a king size tub, big enough for ten plus me!

is sick of looking at Cookie flirting with the local teachers.

can't believe she is allergic to being home.

is wondering why Crazy Kevin did not appear at the party, despite saying he would love to?

doesn't want to hear another sound...

is in San Diego without Zuzana, although she's is in LA with a Japanese guy.

is the most hated woman in Dungannon.

thinks that you just don't get it, do you... I am in love with you... and that won't change over a fight that I want to end already! :(

is amazed at people's lack of morals, what happened to girl power!

thinks I spoke too soon.

is a little broken hearted about leaving Mykonos. Argh!

says: 'John I love you, you can knock me out if you want, I just want you'.

is glad it's all sorted out... for the moment.

knows that you know my confidence is easily broken to build up your ego, don't worry, I know shit you would love to know—I've taken my wallet and keys!

is always the bridesmaid never the bride!

is beginning to see how much he's fucked everything up!

... and the award for the best lie goes to you!

is every negative word in the dictionary today :-(

is wondering what she would be doing now if she was still travelling the globe.

can't seem to shake 'TWATS' today...!

is trying to work out who are his friends and who is not, its interesting!

wants some contact!

is not happy and is going be bored next week as I have no work... a lady of leisure, oh well!

is getting a little bit fed up with Huston!

thought I was... I'm not! :(

is cursing herself for not checking her bloody pockets before putting the clothes in the wash. Damn tissues!

is wishing he had a teleporter to take him where wants to be the most!

stepped on his PS3 controller... there goes 100 bucks.

is in a relationship with a mongoose.

can't wait to sort her hair out! Bring back the blonde!

is sick again... seriously can I have one week without being injured or sick?

wants to go overseas so bad...

is wondering when is he going to have enough money to start partying again!?

just wants you, no one else!

is pissed off someone stole her iPod touch.

has a knack for throwing fuel on a fire!

is back in Poland and hating life!

wants to go travelling sooo bad.

is having a bad Sunday... :-(

got lose in Byron last night with the entire group and it was great. You guys are the best group ever, will miss you loads.

is thinking of legitimate ways to get back in the convent.

is guessing it will never stop... so just accept it and move on!

wants to go back and start all over again.

is extremely angry and upset, and can't believe that someone stole my handbag out of my car!

wants to bang his head against a wall.

is wondering how she's going to survive!?

lives in a big and empty house... anyone want to move in?

is accepting the fact that she is home and will stay there for a few more weeks.

has had a bad day at work and my laptops just broken, arrgghh.

is thinking its all wrong!

is wondering why do I always do the wrong thing?

wishes he couldn't think...

is pissed off that he has to go back to the shite that is commonly known as USA life, yup, he's totally fucked off with the fact he's going back this Saturday...

is ... WTF?

is wondering what a chair would look like if our knees were on the back of our legs?

is sickened by the amount of camel toe she has just witnessed by the joggers today. Put it away!

didn't want a fully functioning rib cage anyway.

is all the worst parts of the bible come true.

wonders what the legal age of consent is in Pan's Neverland, and the implications that may have for sex tourism.

is thinking left handed people should grow up.

is still laughing at what I overheard: 'The bouncer was having a go at me because he thought I was being sick'... 'yeah, the bastard had a go at me too because I stole his drink.'

is putting explosive remote controlled devices in the chests of his entire cartel. Turn states evidence mother fuckers. Go on, I dare you...

is thinking that if we were old Austrian men we would keep our kids in the dark about sex education...

is missing her tonsils and her camera but is delighted with the timing of both losses!

is drawing ducks on walls and pretending to feed them after being forced to listen to Mix 102.3 at work!

wants to know what happened to the midget that jumped out the window?

is on top of the world looking down on creation and the only explanation I can find is...

is shifting shape into a silver wolf and gnawing on her throne of bones.

shouldn't have tried to cut the string with a pickaxe.

is wanting to know where Baz would have driven the lorry full of Pikey's if the keys had been in it?

is thinking that Dave's last meal before we fry him should involve something in Commerce City...

is enjoying no such pineapple action!

knows that Pebble Shit is completely useless, but it's really easy, you're just all too fucking lazy to read the instructions...

is trying to apologise, your so ugly when you cry, please... just cut it out.

has just watched Rambo and wants to kill someone, haha.

is in shock that someone he knows is only going to row around the huge ice-cube that is Antarctica... Yes only Antarctica, where it will be dark for four months!

will regurgitate, eat it and freak you.

is t'was I who fucked the dragon, fuck a life, I fuck a you and if you try and fuck with me then I shall fuck you too.

didn't mean to throw Marie's phone in the Harbour yesterday. Sorry.

is the pony that turned into Pegasus.

is on Roatan, and can't believe Tobias got a Ferrari for passing his final school examinations.

is sorry for spilling KY all through Bilbo's car and writing her name on his windscreen with the heel of her shoe... Oh dear...

is watching Waking the Dead wearing Birkenstock's, with Mick Jagger. Next week: Midsomer Murders and those shoes you send off for in the Sunday supplements.

has realised I am not the nicest person after some beers, I actually came home and beat my wife!

is home from the whales' vagina.

loves Paddy and Jenny, knows how to cut the pineapple, Mia is my best friend, and I fuck rubber ducks.

is you want a cock in your hair band and your pen haahaa Stacey...

is the suicide note left on your answering machine by someone who got the wrong person?

is a male lesbian.

wishes she gave birth to Emma Griffith's!

is just remembering eating Janelle's underwear... Oh my god.

is not sure how the formation of a Ribbon lake will ever come into use in later life.

spiked himself... (its more embarrassing than anything)...

is ready to take lives like the Fed's did Brendan.

has her mother's eyes... they're in her pocket!

is every black woman's white friend.

asks: On a hot summer night, would you offer your throat to the wolf with the red roses?

is WKD Blue today.

thinks if this were the 1700's the Olsen twins would have been burned at the stake for being witches.

is loving that she's entering the Hospitality industry with a passionate hate for the human race.

doesn't hate the sky just because he doesn't have wings.

is the anti-flipper.

had a wicked day with my peanut! Didn't wanna leave!

is the future, you are the past and the present is the sword I clutch in my hands...

thinks 'Ribena, I know what you're drinking' is the most annoying line ever.

is going to start saying quarter after five like those from Canada, instead of quarter past five.

bleuuuuurgh. ouch. amazing.

is blind. Her carer has only a thumb and a finger. Retarded.

pissed on Leighton last night in the club, so Chick smacked him, haha so funny, and then he feel asleep while shaggin' a bird.

is drugs, rock and roll, bad ass Vegas hoes, late night booty calls, shining disco balls!

got out of the wrong side of the bed and liked it!

is... wanting to kill someone!

says Amy breathe on your own, you've done it for 25 years, don't stop now.

is shaking, baking and figure eighting.

is the gin in the gin-soaked girl.

is proud for Bok van Blerk and that he is a real bore. Pain and suffering has to STOP!

despises pollen... bastards!

is looking at the moths, there is no humping involved and no eye contact, I don't understand.

has had enough of life on the surface and is moving under the sea.

is going to become a dog whisperer!

hopes his spaceship knows which way to go to get out of bed.

is ha cools light is like a pillow fight.

wonders: do you think mushrooms are cool-looking?

is gonna free the people with the plank of love by the fire of death.

thinks a couple of bitches in his life are so stupid... I'm about to leave all red like a portion of chips...

is shooting up poetry.

knows its kinda nasty at 2am... but I don't care if the kids are watching, I am it, like motherfuckin coffee cream and sugar, girls love sugar.

is usually drunk usually sex usually heart.

is a masterpiece... if you think I couldn't handle her, then you really are mistaken. You have seen my demeanor, I had to control myself.

is turning orange again!

completely understands that sleep is the cousin of death. Oh what nice relations you have Mr. Death.

is the twelfth Cyclops.

thinks funerals are insane, as the chicks are so horny. It's like fishing with dynamite!

is really tired lately due to her boyfriend hitting her in his sleep!

has seen a pig with Wellington boots. Priceless!

is still sitting in the roof thing and nearly got eaten yesterday by a small boy!

the new face of Fanny.

is laughing at Hepatitis B, come and get me you Schmuk!

has committed a 178... die-fly-die!

is welcoming you to Shitvac, your life is about to demise into an exercise and a sunlight free version of an insomniac's rendition of 'how to learn Uni in six days'.

was living in a forest with witches.

is too weird to live and too rare to die.

thinks that not all blind people are in wheelchairs, think about it guys!

is a Zombie God.

has seriously worked it out! Under Matt's anger and tightly-brushed hair he IS really Roxanne! Think about it... constantly brushes hair = wig. FACT. Remember where you heard it first.

is needing a big hug

is long gone and disappointed in himself for believing in her once again… I am getting ready to go back home and at least attempt to have some peace of mind…

is looking at his text message and wondering what exactly he means by that?

is thinking what a tosser. Why would he?

is pissed off she won't get to see the gorgeous Paul on Saturday night… how about breakfast on Sunday?

is seriously fed up with being lectured!

is rippin' stuff out. She has pissed him off.

is at the airport about to board his plane and is missing his girl already.

is getting on with MY life, pity other people tried to stick their noses in.

is losing the will to live.

wants a Ross!

is finding it hard to believe it's nearly been one year since his beloved granddad passed away! Miss you!

is so over that slag!

said good bye to the folks yesterday… boo hoo!

is saying OMG some people really do change… for the worse…

wants to walk in Hyde Park with her loved one again :(

is sad but life goes on.

is tired, tired, tired and seems to be getting sadder by the hour - don't go Katarina.

is trying really hard this time.

is saying you are a dick… you of all people! Why?

wishes people would be a little more considerate and a little less self absorbed.

is feeling blue, when he can't see you.

wants to know when life got so complicated.

is washing her hands of it.

wants Kim back NOW!

is missing Princess Sunnybomb already!

is going to miss her Christian :(

is asking why do people like to play with peoples emotions all the time?

is glad he still rings me on a nightly basis.

can't believe she broke her ring from Amsterdam! Shattered!

is crying me a river.

feels like he's never been away… oh, and that's not a good thing!

is not knowing how to feel at this stage about her jewellery being stolen… I'm sure it will kick in soon…

is wondering why are you so difficult? Well it's your loss.

misses her pirate! She needs a hug…

wonders where the f&%k is Ryan?! Come back…

is gutted that the boy band she used to think were hot, now either aren't or are clearly gay, I want to be young again when life was simple.

is sad that some friends forget about you, but those great ones stick by you through thick and thin.

is wishing I could tell you how I feel about you.

is having a shitty day :(

is saying sorry, but you talk to every girl exactly the same…

really wants to know… do you think I was born yesterday? You total fuck wit! *ANGRY*

is thinking you are both so sad, I feel sorry for you… so stupid…

says you do my head in :(

is saying you had it coming.

says "What am I?… everything you are not…"!

is not sure what to believe anymore!

wants to go home now!

is homesick and heartbroken that I've lost my Greenstone and this time it hasn't come back to me.

gets no answer so the question still remains.

is hoping for a bit of good news…

sends her thoughts and best wishes to all of Danny's family and friends. Such a sad loss but many happy memories.

is out of the game until July.

is wishing the Swedes could have stayed longer!

says you ruined my day… your being sooo out of order and you know most of the stuff you said isn't true… just please get out of my life and don't talk to me.

thinks tall Jen is malicious.

is hoping against hope that is all goes well this evening!

never thought it would be you.

is going to miss Lucy, Tommy, Adam, Hannah, Amy, Chris, Stacy, Jamie, Dane, Euan, the kangaroos, the didgeridoo players, the seagulls, the sun, Wakeup…

is thinking not again… WTF?

wants to understand why pricks turn out to be bigger pricks!

is sick of people's bullshit!

just wants things to be simple…

is thinking now who's gonna cuddle me and keep me warm at night.

believes the Rudder has fallen off and the honeymoon is over.

is not so sure anymore.

is a dumbarse… I thought you knew me better… I love you.

is in a sad mood, his boy has left today to go on his own path… not a good day.

is heartbroken and homesick.

is back in Hatfield and hating it :(

needs someone to cuddle and hold.

is saying you are blaming me Emma? I am on my ass myself! You are evil stuff; you have been saying you love me? Yeah whatever!

wants his best friend back.

is upset about losing her diamond ring… has anyone seen it?

knew sorries just wouldn't do it.

is :(It'll all get better in time.

wants to know who stole her dogs AND who broke into her car last night!

is going crazy with thoughts… don't know what the outcome will be?

thinks your both little wankers.

is sad that he can't be jetting off also!

found woman in black UNREAL… shit scary though… not really sure what's going on… cuddle please?

is strolling in a field with grass, wanting to hold someone's hand…

doesn't know how to stop the tears.

is really pissed off, but shouldn't be a bit surprised.

wants a cuddle from him :(

is back in town... his home town! Let's see what happens, hey?

is realistic about the situation.

is wallowing in his boiler pity.

is thinking that hugs outweigh anything.

had an adversarial conversation with his mum, and now misses her... a lot...

is thinking now he probably shouldn't have sent that sms!

wants a cuddle please. Thank you.

is =[You are the definition of a twat!

says I love you and I really hope it will never happen again.

is amused - just found out my ex-fiancée is marrying a stripper in November... lucky escape!

is letting you all know Daniel McClymont officially gets my deadly silence treatment for one week - BITCHHOEFACELIAR... I think you are very rude!

is getting out of here

is finishing work on Friday, ugly people will no longer be beautified! Greece here I come!

is going to Marbella - lock up your daughters!

will this day next week be in Galway, where the place stinks of dried seaweed... ah good times.

is so excited about spending Spring Break in the US of A.

is partying in Ibiza next month! Woooo...

is thinking about the good times to come in South Africa!

is going back to England for a holiday at the end of August!

is getting ready for her six month adventure.

is getting prepared for the biggest adventure of his life. Argentina to Alaska bitches...

is coming to America!

is off to Alicante! Woop woop :)

has just booked a luxury suite at the Venetian! Viva Las Vegas baby!

is heading for NYC.

is planning some sort of maggot snow trip this fall.

thinks this road trip is going to be wicked sideburns.

is on her way to Beverly Hills!

is leaving for Miami tomorrow and she can't fucking wait. Bring on the ring of fire...

is planning a trip back to Oz with Therese!

finally has enough frequent flier points to book his Asia trip!

is getting pumped about going to Sri Lanka!

is back home in London :(but not for long as Espanyol awaits my arrival :)

is going around the world so I can find my baby.

is not just going to Boston, Niagara is now on the trip :-)

has just handed in her notice and is started to plan the next travelling adventure. Any one want to come?

is getting ready to go back on the road.

is gone 'till November.

still hasn't got his ticket to come home as the travel agent has fucked up.

is going to Greece on Tuesday for Elliot's sisters wedding.

is starting to plan a holiday - those of you Down Under might see me there about October-time.

is packing lots of jumpers for the UK.

is packing her bags and leaving New South Wales. Queensland here I come.

has decided to start planning her next trip with her free time... hmmmm...

is off to Spain on Thursday! Leaving on a jet plane, don't know when I'll be back again!

is finally leaving France on Sunday, excellent.

is going to Guernsey, then Newcastle, then Sussex!

is scared about hers and Christine's trip.

cant wait for New Zealand!

is looking at flights unsuccessfully.

is in denial. I have a 5am AND a layover tomorrow.

is on her way to the North of the South.

is finally getting a small vacation for me! A long weekend in Turin.

will be in Melbourne shortly to say hi to your mum.

is going to Israel next week. Any ideas?

is flying to San Francisco tomorrow!

is planning things to do with his next three weeks in Ireland…

is off again, this time Carlsbad!

is staying in England for longer than expected… stupid American visa!

is sitting on her suitcase and pondering… why doesn't her life fit into one single suitcase?

is fighting with the entire airport to get on a fucking plane to Tahiti.

is out of here… Victoria here I come!

is gone baby, gone.

is on his way to Panama city, the one in Florida this time.

is getting ready to leave Cairns in the morning and head to Alice Springs - No more work and lots of play!

is going to have a look at the rainforest.

is getting geared up for Hong Kong… oh what a beautiful creature!

is off to the Dominican with Dominika for some sunshine…

is going to Whyalla today! Yay!

has very itchy fucking feet!

is excited about going to Poland on Friday!

is going to Kangaroo Island for the long weekend.

is wondering if San Francisco, Hollywood, Venice Beach, San Diego, and Las Vegas is ready for this?

is planning a road trip around Ireland for September, and anyone who wants to, can come.

is taking off for Portugal tomorrow.

is going to the place where everything is legal.

is off for a weekend of judo in Scotland, and then holidays here he comes :)

is hanging out to go to Canada.

has one foot on the plane…

is off to Thailand next Friday to meet her family! Yay!

is heading to Paradise… Surfers that is.

is moving back to Cusco. But is in shock that she has just had a friend request from Maria Grant.

is cruising over to Tasmania with Hinton - ooh get in!

flies away tomorrow!

is off to Oktoberfest in Germany… to drink Weiss beer.

is leaving on a jet plane. Destination: Switzerland!

is off to Fiji in the morning. For six weeks of bliss!

is in the middle of booking a Contiki America tour? Got to love staff discounts.

is off in to Newcastle with Ben, Sam, Hollie and Lisa, holiday hunting / shopping / beer gardening…

is packed and ready for action! Hopefully he will return?

can't wait until this time on Friday when she will be landing in Los Angeles.

is going to miss, miss, miss her girls… what will I do without you all for so long?

just picked up his tickets for his holiday, but wants to go now.

is happy… Vietnam is calling.

is in Melbourne waiting to catch his plane to go on his holiday.

is going to Brazil. DeArne I'm going to miss you, but I know you are going to rep our ends in S-Town!

is reflecting

is thinking what an awesome weekend he just had, but don't cry because it's over, smile because it happened.

thinks days like today put everything into perspective. Live each day to the full.

is back at Micah's palace in Surfers Paradise, just like the good ole times, eh?

doesn't understand why all good things must come to an end… Manchester is sorely missed…

is heading back to Whistler after an emotional farewell.

was in New York this day last year! Where has it all gone wrong?

is reflecting on the events of the week… some exciting, some tough…

cannot believe that it is three years since he went to Australia.

is missing the Stebbings sisters today after looking at my pictures!

fucking loved seeing Karen.

is still smiling about the weekend… really wanna get a rewind :(

is laughing at last nights antics!

is never going to forget this year. She misses everyone so much already!

is back in Londontown, but missing her Jew family lots!

is thinking a few Corona's on the beach... in Mexico... that could be nice...

wants it to be last Sunday again.

is wishing she was back in San Sebastian again!

has had a lovely weekend, although it started with a shocker... performing first aid on a man hit by a car.

is dreaming of Sydney and beers on the beach at Coogee...

is missing "callipos" and warm nights.

had such an awesome time in Scotland... you know, back in the day!

is missing her travelling friends!

is about to go get a tribal tattoo to remind her of the good times in New Zealand!

thinks it's all over... Burnside will never be the same again...

is getting old and saying to all his friends: 'Thanks, I love you'!

had a fabulous day out with Carol and Cliona yesterday - thanks guys!

is wishing I was back in Egypt with my gorgeous man!

went to see an Irish dancing competition and has decided she really really misses it.

is smiling as she looks through all the travelling pictures. Good times!

is thinking its been a whole year since me and Louisa left on our amazing trip!

is still laughing at Armitage and the drag queens...

loved the sea, vines & Victoria weekend.

is back from Israel. She wants to go back. Miss it so much.

wants to be out travelling again.

is thinking that last night was fun and amazing!

has just been laughing with J.Q. about the amazing craic we had on the West coast.

is thinking about this time last year!

has had an awesome two days...

is missing Berlin but looking forward to going back again in a few months—fingers crossed!

very much enjoyed T-Bone Thursday.

is remembering all the good times from the Wine Club. WC4life.

is missing those afternoon naps in the Redmill right now, and has finally moved all her stuff.

wants to says thanks a million girls for such a fun weekend.

is reflecting that this day a year ago was when he left to go on his adventure around the world…!

had the best night, and he knows you loved it too so don't lie :-)

is still smiling about last night :)

is back home with a bang! Big up to Dane and his boys for a sick tour!

forgot how much he likes Krish and Michelle!

is wishing she was running around Spain with Josefin again…

has just looked at the videos from the mass! OMG I miss all you girls so much.

is back, but really loves Dublin and wishes she had stayed there for the weekend.

wishes that he was drinking a cold beer on a hot day while watching the cricket at Adelaide Oval!

is back in Ireland with no job, no money and no regrets!

would much prefer to be on his bike in Thailand.

is thinking man oh man what a night… ahh the memories… nothing better than getting ya groove on…

cant believe how good Gatecrasher was! Intense, raw emotion!

is all about *'Now that's what I call music 1993'*.

had a wicked night with the guys and girls from Iceland… going to miss Brenda and Terry loads!

is reflecting on what was a good, but truly genuine random night out.

had the worst weekend ever, but all getting great now. Perfect.

is pretty sure that was the strangest weekend ever.

disagrees that the tally says twelve… she did NOT come on to a Swedish man, it just happens that 'I like your bum' is the only Swedish she knows. Good times, eh?

is loving themselves right now

is on the crest of a wave and I am going to surf this bad boy the whole way…

is the best words in the best order.

is still by far the most qualified person that you'll ever know.

is as good as it gets.

is the dogs bollox.

is going to be paying himself dividends soon. In a Philip Green stylee.

looks in the mirror and sees a soldier...

is sofa king good.

knows everything I am not, is making me everything I am.

is a true entrepreneur!

is old-skool cool... like a leather jacket!

is saying walk with me now and you'll fly with me later.

is slicking it out.

is congratulating himself on being the best.

is saying don't be jealous of me.

feels like she is on top of the world.

is pretty good thanks.

is a brilliant cook after all that...

has been to the gym all week, and is now looking like an extra from *300*.

is better than you!

is AMAZING...

is pretty much a cruise control sorta guy.

has the biggest brain, do you dare to challenge?

is this generations Richard Branson... only far, far better!

is schmicked up!

is a legend in his own lunch-time.

is the man.

is way too cool for school.

is most definitely gods favourite.

signed up for eBay... watch out world!

is probably as close to perfection as any human being could ever be. Yes she definitely thinks so!

is at his peak, its all down hill from here!

is wiggida, wiggida wicked awesome.

is hard to beat.

is Astro man, the first rays of the new rising sun.

has just carbon off-set her flight home and feels damn good about it.

is loving his new hair cut…

is funny as fuck!

is the sexiest man in Ibiza, and is hot, hot, hot!

is on top of the world…

will suffocate your sense of disbelief.

is harder, better, stronger, faster.

is the newest member of the Bratpack…

has a foxy new girlfriend.

is at the top of the list.

is new and improved… with even less to lose.

is going to ace it! Woop woop!

says it's all about having the right attitude.

is so fly he's getting called G5.

is in love with Oliver Morgan.

is breathing like a star.

is going to be the star of Oceans 14.

is kind of a big deal around here, people know me!

loves the way the money goes clickity-clank into his piggy bank…

is Clapham's best kept secret.

is a smart material.

rates his negotiation skills as "successful" at the moment.

is the 2008 McGuyvor…

was always cool, so Blaize lower your pieces!

is staying on his A game!

is a man, with a plan… I got five on it.

is as smooth as sandpaper. Not.

is taking on the world.

feels so good she wants to jump back and kiss her self.

is rich I tell ya, RICH!

is the new Fonze for the new world.

does exactly what it says on the tin...

is so fly for a white guy.

saved the crazy bus lady's life! That's right people... I'm a hero!

is a jolly good fellow.

is a force, a constant source, oh yes he is a shining light.

is ready... born ready...

always knew he would see his name up on the big screen.

is busy being a radster.

is Good, Good, Good...!

has made her mommy proud today.

is thinking "Rome wasn't built in a day... but I wasn't on that particular job!"

is great! Fucking great!

is practising her pout.

is singing *'Yesterday'* and it sounds much better than the Beatles ever did.

is slickin' it out.

THE EVENT.

is touching the sky.

is gonna be the best looking super hero ever!

is probably doing something more interesting than you.

is whatever I wanna be.

is the happiest person in the room!

will take a bow.

is singing Cathy is coool.

is sticking it up there for all the world to see, you know, just in case...

is wondering why there is no water all of a sudden, and wishing that she'd already showered, cleaned her teeth and filled the kettle.

is laughing! How can you not feel an iPod when you put your jeans in the washing?

is hating this getting home in near pitch blackness shit...

has just been star gazing and it was bloody hilarious!

is apologizing if he poisoned anyone with mercury that he spilled all over the lab...

has forgiven Miss Moret, after all a platypus is a very attractive animal!

is not what he seems.

thinks that Aussie's don't know what a real shop is, all I wanted was a bloody pair of shoes!

is concerned with his and McGregor's sudden fascination with Jack the Ripper...

wishes he had legs like Giulia Borracci.

is choosing her gown for ze wedding of Barbara ze Great...

is hoping he can still swing it both ways at pace!

is working out how to get Angelica in a 'gotcha call'... any ideas will be welcomed...

wants Lindsey to smile :)

is trying to organise every piece of junk she has accumulated over the past two years.

is maintaining my desire.

is playing some good poker but needs to stay away from the on-line roulette.

has just cleaned his car and is now having a beer, but can't go out! No, no, no.

is getting up early... again... ish.

went to buy some work pants and ended up with two suits.

is all excited about her volunteer work with the Wallabies! Aww they are gonna be so cute!

would like to wish Duncan the best, but would appreciate if he found alternative representation!

is the biggest procrastinator in the world.

is only slightly amused at Barry's sense of humour.

thinks I don't know what it is but I want it!

is watching Eurovision, and loving the English commentary! What a laugh.

is sad because his little kitten Fiddy was in pain today when his little nuts were cut out after his hit-and-run!

has a hippy head… but not a hippy body, yet…

wishes the fairies would magically clean her room for her.

is telling you to come to the bus stop and bring an umbrella.

is dismissing Raine's claim that he invented the Tamagotchi.

plans to get back all the money she lost on Tuesday - things are looking good!

is caught in the middle of an African conflict!

is thinking the flu shot was a waste of time.

is watching the chickens trying to peck Sherry's freckles off!

has said goodbye western power, and kicked it in the guts.

is already sick of having hooks in his mouth.

is not ready to explain to Coffee… he's over 18 and should know exactly what to do…!

paid $21 for a helicopter - Bargain!

is going on a European Tour. Who would have thought that!

was in awe of Lorraine Dunne's dance moves last night.

has just discovered his neighbours have unsecured wireless Internet! Free Internet for me! Oh Yes!

is ready for it, whatever it turns out to be!

can't believe the big man's vast array of ridiculous shit.

is telling you that you should see their faces when they see this robot can move!

thinks Philipp is easy!

is saying calm yourself down women…!

just had the publicity shots for our Channel 4 documentary about me and my family out in July.

is now banister-less.

wonders if she made a mistake at the hairdressers yesterday? It's a bit dark!

is a karaoke machine… unlike Anja.

is back but not in action…!

just doesn't understand how some people have managed to succeed in business!

is thinking Ashton Kutcher is too good looking… bastard!

can drive again in five days. And is still laughing over Jenny buying him batteries and a Kitkat.

is thinking about his little protégé prankster.

looks like he has something to hide…

is finding mixing music quite tricky.

has gone to be touched for one whole hour, and all paid for.

is loving his new name.

is wondering if women really are from Venus or do they just act that way!?

is saying we're just friends.

is back in Sydney… after two weeks in the Queensland bush looking after Wallabies and Kangaroos!

has a bruise on her cheek from Karin's biting.

is remembering that time he wasn't pasty white.

is not sure how she woke up with a headache since she was on driving duties last night.

will chase you for the flight money!

is going to shock everyone with my new hair style… hope you like it because it's short!

is coming to terrorise a library near you.

wonders if Keith found the mastermind behind the hair straightener posters put up all over the gym? No. 1 suspect: Paul the Chin.

is like a bwooberry.

looks around and sees angels in the architecture.

is having a very "blonde" morning.

is wondering why the inside of Golden Gaytimes isn't nearly as satisfying as the outside…

is not that confident in Alison's quitting ability… all the best darling!

wants another piercing… suggestions please?

is still a Brazilian sari wearing smoker.

is definitely positive that today is the day.

is skint… she'll contact everyone on Tuesday when she gets paid and can afford credit and Internet!

is part of the silent majority.

wishes that she was born into the Amazonian 'untouched tribe'.

is making a kite out of a Cornflakes box!

does not a hero make!

is going to be Freddy Mercury tonight, Mathew.

's jaw is on the floor that her old school friend is married with two kids to a middle aged foreign man!

is loading music onto Nonye and Clare the Bear's iPod's! Painful exercise!

's best friend isn't Michelle Comerton but a lady called Therese Clarke.

is looking for a ruby in a mountain of rock.

thinks he has a good coach when it comes to shopping, 100% strike rate!

is straight… I promise!

thinks that with the improvements in science and technology that they should've invented sleep injections!

is a Mexican / lumber jack.

is shocked as she cannot believe a nine year old Chinese BOY was just searching for 'hottest Zac Efron pic's' on the Internet next to her!

needs a hobby for the summer, any suggestions?

is on the train and is blown away that his phone can go on the net.

hails to the pool ball oracle.

is going to get his own back on the people who stitched him up at Sharon and Bernie's by making him dance with the thing!

is wondering… who sucked the colour out of Sheffield?

is now an expert silver miner and mountain biker.

asks: Who is this Patrick Walsh?

is thinking it would have been a good idea to go to the toilet before the plumbers started to rip them up…

thinks Adam is a bit of a knob… bring back the Prince of Arabela!

is having a laugh tonight! It's Trouble in Clowntown!

has Blue Cheese exclusive to Barney's.

is dosed up the eye balls and all because of a cold!

is the original salad spoon!

is wondering if Swish should change their name to the Slovakia Brothers.

doesn't want to sit next to you on the tram!

is no longer in trouble.

will be thinking of Colin on Monday when his bizarre love triangle comes to a head at "We Love Sounds"…

is gonna keep on keepin' on.

is completely broke thanks to her Internet spending spree.

is at home… getting me some monies at the good old gapsted!

will definitely not buy a motorbike - I promise!

is gonna win big on the horses today and then win the lottery tonight.

has been in Brixton and bumped into a few crackheadz along the way, much to his surprise. Not!

is so embarrassed that I'm creasing up you joker.

has ruled out plane / train spotting as a potential hobby, thanks for suggestions Jacqueline!

is not gonna pander to Neanderthals today.

dares Kirsten / Sarah to try something, I will always win (Sarah don't change, its funnier this way).

is the king of the analogue camera... I'm gonna keep it alive.

had the funniest day ever! A little sister has been beaten to death with a yoga ball :D

is getting restless now that it's nearly over!

is ready... are you?

wishes he hadn't been to the dentists.

is not a huge fan of interpretive dance and has spent most of this evening confused.

is clearly not an idiot!

is pumped to face another day. At least that's what I'm telling myself anyway.

has a hotel stay in Derry for four people to give away. It has to be used before the end of August!

is playing guitar, not guitar hero, guitar.

has bad toothache and as a result her teeth are sad.

is having to pick her jaw up off the floor after hearing the fantastic news - this calls for a bottle of Pinot!

thinks it's so good when it hits your lips.

is not looking forward to getting his hearing checked out tomorrow... What?

is still more than a lil freaked, by Chris's big toe!

lost his phone again... please send me your digits.

is fucking Matt Damon.

is well on the way to discovering the ultimate destiny of the universe!

is in love... with a fictional character... again.

is looking for new friends to get to know.

is in a love triangle between Emily and Jessica.

shouldn't have sang so much last night.

is now with action utility belt and super duper... um... stuff...!

is so proud of Officer Patel!

is amazed at how much trouble she gets herself in to with Ian.

is getting closer with her Glasto shopping list... next up: Fanny pack!

thinks his thumb is in serious strife.

is gonna "man up."

is not paralyzed but seems to be struck by you...

just got a Carlie Bruni-esque haircut.

is wondering whether the move should be for money or emotional well-being?

is back to being a blonde... phew... after lots of blood, sweat and maybe a few *sniff-sniffs*.

is gonna bring back acid techno!

is so bored I've even resorted to cooking for myself to give me something to do!

thought I'd got rid of the big cockroach in the kitchen, only to discover another tonight... must have called in back up - damn those pesky creatures!

is being cheeky

is giving you David Beckham's number: 077XXXXXXXXX. Go ahead and give him a call, you know he wants to talk to you...

has an intellectual inferiority complex (which is actually quite simple)...

is sick of women undressing him with their eyes and making sex noises. I'm taken, O.K! Find another sex symbol to fantasize about!

went to a meeting today for premature ejaculators. I left early...

is laughing at... "they are well-bread homosapians, with large aortic pumps" (good people with big hearts, thesaurus translation).

is thinking, with friends like these who needs armies.

wants to congratulate his lil bro for passing his driving test... and pass the chauffeurs cap on to him!

has not had a hair cut in six months and it's kinda growing on me!

is thinking the dictionary needs to be revised. Word.

is keeping a beat with no metronome, no metronome...

wants to hop on the good foot and do the bad thing.

says save water this summer… have a shower with me.

… have you seen this man? <=--<<

is eating some chocolate mousse from Marks & Spencer. Verdict 9/10 - pot could have been bigger.

loves "No Armani no Punani… No Spray no Lay"… got to love the toilet attendant's rhymes to get you to put on aftershave!

is not happy with himself for always repeating things, repeating things, repeating things, repeating things…

needs to clone himself… again… with an accountant this time, and not a builder!

is denying everything until I see my solicitor.

has just done it… your move now…

is actually a hula hoop would champion, but I didn't want to be recognised so I just let it drop… felt it to be unfair to the others, I would have been there all night swirling that thing!

is upstairs for drinking, downstairs for dancing, in the middle for romancing.

attended the ceremony 'Unhanging of the Glass'. He feels it should be hung back up!

is going to have to make some changes

is in utter disbelief at his own behaviour, he hates alcohol more than he enjoys it, but yet what still happens… to anyone that still cares, I am truly sorry!

is wondering how long it takes stress to kill you.

has without doubt, wasted the year.

is wishing for less shite all around!

needs to get her act together and stop faffing.

is getting drunk by himself on a Monday… how sad!

is counting down until the end…

should probably just move into the liquor store and get it over with.

is thinking that tomorrow will be a good day… she hopes.

isn't too sure anymore…

will not be smiling again until December 2009.

is thinking things can only get better... still!

wants to break free.

is happy to see she is not the only one who achieved nothing this weekend...

wonders will she get a warning before her head explodes?

is the wrong side of something!

is wanting something different and exciting to happen.

is losing the will to live...

needs to get out of this place...

is needing to find some willpower.

thinks it's time to move on.

is not sure how she feels, but knows its not good.

has no will whatsoever... why is that?

is so unbelievably bored! What a boring day I've had! Someone please help me!

is ready to throw the towel in. It really is almost time.

doesn't understand much about life lately...

is crap and has no self-control when it comes to a certain something!

is needing to put a stop to my spending!

breathes it in and breathes it out... it's not a habit; its cool...

is thinking... shots or work?

is very rich in fashion assets and very poor in financial assets.

has to stop waking up in the middle of the night and getting dressed for work!

is not in the least bit motivated.

can feel a glitch in the entire system... something is definitely not right with me...

is thinking it's like moving mountains.

just doesn't know what to do with herself.

is praying for the end of time to hurry up and arrive.

needs some vava voom in his life... but would settle for some zoom zoom!

is feeling all depressed. Can things really get any worse?

can't pay the rent... 'cause all the money is spent.

is making some bad decisions before his big day at the library tomorrow.

doesn't know what's going on… and then some.

's world is falling apart. Things can't get any worst at the moment.

is hoping for a better day.

is a lazy bum… *yawns*… and can't be arsed to keep on packing.

is thinking what do I do?

needs to muster up some serious work ethic… really soon…

is wanting to chill.

thinks some decisions are better left unmade!

is glugging Merlot wine to aid the falling into sleep.

is so confused, I don't know what to do.

is having a lonely night preparing for Jäegerbomb: The Return.

has issues that need addressing… sharpissssshhhhh.

is confused… 15 Pro Plus and four litres of Dr Pepper… why can't I sit still?

is not going to self destruct.

should actually be doing something… but clearly won't.

is a proud owner of a new phone… yes he lost another one!

can't do this any longer.

is not liking the state of everything! It's horrible!

has had enough of this!

is thinking "Hmmm this is a first… I don't want to party, but I kind of have to."

still doesn't know what to do!

is so lazy she has to motivate herself to motivate herself…

is fed up with wanting things so badly.

is wondering what does having a life feel like again?!

has too much shit to do and can't be arsed doing any of it!

is getting so annoyed at tipping winners but not betting anything.

never knows what she's doing… back there.

is actually pretty knackered.

thanks the lord that she's another week closer to the end!

is a couple of days behind... March already? What happened to February?

apologies if her whining offended Lina... it is just that she is used to being in a far superior country to this.

wonders if his week could get any worse!

is tired today, too much work and not enough sleep.

thinks the only good thing out of today was I now have enough status points for free club membership!

is thinking I don't know what to do with myself.

can only try his best.

is on laptop number four!

wrote 'Eloise is totally detoxing this week'... on Monday! Yeah right!

is starting to think that red wine could be a cure for a cold! Now all I need to do is sleep...

needs to get the fuck out of here!

is counting days until life starts!

is thinking she probably shouldn't have just spent 200 bucks on shoes and clothes... but oops too late!

says it's not illegal unless you get caught. Right?!

is going to get fucked tonight.

is sat wondering what the hell to do.

has already fallen off the non drinking wagon...

is wishing she didn't have insomnia :(

is planning for Thursday night were it begins by getting lashed and ends with having a blaze with my girl.

is weighed down by bubbles and dreams.

is tired and pissed, what's new...

has bailed on study and is joining her friends in town... good old Alcopops are doing the trick.

is on a road to nowhere.

has work, work, work and not enough play, play, play.

is skating on thin ice.

hasn't slept at all... my brain thinks too much!

is a bit bruised... stupid doors!

has heaps of shit to do today, and probably isn't gonna do any of it! What you gonna do about it?

is wondering why nothing is ever simple?

is hanging her head in shame...

hates it when you say you are going to save money, and then go and spend £160 on shots...

is well and truly over it... and it hasn't even begun!

wishes all the stress would go away... help :(

is wanting a weekend off...

has figured out all the things he'd rather be doing and none of them correlate with what he is actually doing.

is bored of this home life... I need to break out. Help me.

is on the road once again, and hates people that lie - you know who you are, I am not happy but never mind I'll just get on with my life, eh. I wish something's were different.

is starting to make changes

is starting fresh: new job, new house, just need a new man and I'll be sorted... yeah OK, singledom suits me just fine for now :)

found a plan of action, now I just got to work on it.

is going to stay positive, even if it depresses him to do so!

is a new person.

is going on a diet after actually becoming an elephant.

thinks the law of attraction is always working!

is sleeping, running, watching movies, seeing friends and family and basically enjoying having free time again.

got her three stone award, yay.

is on a detox since he didn't drink yesterday... don't know how long it will last though!

is getting her life back on track.

hasn't drunken any booze for 18 days!

is determined to lose weight by the time he goes to Greece.

has at the age of 23 finally decided he has ambitions!

is building bridges and getting the F' over them!

is ready to get involved in her first well behaved weekend in a while...

knows that a change is going to come.

is taking a night off the booze as his body is fucked.

has removed all the crap from her floor and even put some of it away!

is done with chasing people.

is a third of the way through the month of no drinking!

is making plans to leave.

feels it's time for a change?

is getting her life together... out with the old...

has decided that this is going to be my final destination, no more sitting round having my time wasted.

is working out a game plan.

has decided to be more positive, and is going skiing in twelve days!

is single... but not for long.

is acting in a professional manner and hoping she has now eradicated the problem.

doesn't know what to make of the changes, time to think hard...

is proud how long she has lasted on her healthy detox!

is ready for a change!

has just entered day three of life with out booze... welcome to detox!

is having a shot at it!

's ready for anything and everything!

is saying fuck Uni and fuck work, he is going to the doctors.

is getting motivated and organised!

is off the booze... not by choice... but still off it!

has gone eight days without booze, impressive.

is a man, with a plan... that's all that matters.

tried so hard, but is not getting positive results... not yet... but she will.

is finding the diet so incredibly hard.

is the proud owner of a clean and healthy liver.

no longer has blue Tuesday syndrome.

is looking forward to what the next seven months will bring and he can't wait!

is taking a step back and thinking about shit.

needed a night off.

is thinking good things will happen!

is glad he did nothing last night!

is learning to stay calm…

has got through his first weekend of not drinking!

is going to follow the advise offered in the *Zeigeist Addendum* movie she just watch on Google.

is totally detoxing this week.

has given up alcohol… having no hangovers is great!

walks along the supposed Golden Path.

is struggling to remain tee-total.

hasn't had any booze for ten days.

is off Hooch for now, if Rebecca can do it so can we.

is going to be healthy and a non drinker…

can snap out of it and deal with it!

is wondering does she have it in her.

is contemplating his next destination…

is dreaming of several things but mostly about the end of the self imposed alcohol ban, weekends are just not the same sober!

is praying for tonight…

has more cunning plans than Cochrane has turnips.

is loving the fact that although it's Friday today and Saturday tomorrow, I have chosen to refrain from any alcohol. Now aren't I a good boy?

is currently living off savings

is laughing at the thought of having to wear a suit tomorrow… wish me luck, I have an interview.

is leading an unemployed but happy life ;>)

is saying please, please, please someone find me a job!

is wondering what she will get asked at her interview tomorrow… and will try to remember to wear trousers.

is scoping out the local job front.

has an interview tomorrow! Woop Woop!

is sleepy from all this work, and is on the job hunt once again and really feeling the heat!

can't wait to start working and get some bloody money!

is on strike until further notice.

got fired today and unfortunately he doesn't even care.

is job hunting the big US of A - bloody boring.

doesn't know quite where to begin with finding recruitment agents and courses… any clues?

is sorted with a house, and pondering what job to go for?

is not looking forward to her five interviews tomorrow. Going to need beer when I'm done!

is looking for another job!

will be a PE teacher as of 25th August.

is unemployable.

has had so many interviews… she now thinks its time that she also had a job!

is job hunting. Does anyone want to employ her?

is starting a new job tomorrow.

will be starting work for the first time in two months! Not happy!

is looking for any work going in Dublin for the next three weeks, let me know and I'll take it! Seriously.

is looking at what she wants to do for a job!

has got me a job… woo hoo! Start on Monday! Bring on the money, baby!

is bored of looking for a job.

is in Texas, got a job for next week, now just need a place to live!

is trying to get back on the grind.

had a very successful interview and is maybe one step closer to employment.

is job hunting, any ideas anyone?

is so happy he has just got a €50,000 a year job and is looking forward starting on Monday!

has landed himself a new job, woo hoo…!

really wants someone to give her a good job!

is starting a new job tomorrow in Dun Laoire sailing club. Woo hoo.

is very happy and excited about getting her new job! Savings have been depleted... severely!

is trying to get this damn qualification

is scared as she starts Uni in four weeks!

is surprisingly excited for starting back at school.

wants to be clever =[

is thinking you're having a f**king laugh? Hating Uni right now! Why can't it just end!

doesn't understand why education tutorials are compulsory when all we do is make sock puppets?

is stressing over Uni work... where are the Uni fairies when you need them?

is thawing out the literary ice age.

is not a fan of regression! Or correlations! Stupid things!

doesn't understand why science is necessary because he can't understand it.

has gone back to school, and misses easy HSC essays.

is glad that it is almost the weekend. Not so glad about the amount of Uni work that needs to be done!

never wants to learn anything about depressive illnesses ever again.

is sick of Medical Law and Ethics!

thinks being stuck in a ditch in Colesburg is much cooler than all the Uni work to be done this week.

is allowed back to school tomorrow.

wonders why would you have a war that lasted 40 years... it just means more to learn!

is in the library reppin', but can't be fucked for school...

can't wait to put her lil dancing peeps through there exams in July!

thinks was that really history? Wow!

is land law land law land law.

is hating acid test, gearing, liquidity, asset turnover and sales turnover ratios!

"doesn't fit into being a typical student."

has a solid 10+ hours of Uni to do today… damn.

is enjoying her last night with a relaxing spa before serious study starts!

has a hot date with a financial accounting assignment… you can feel my excitement.

is trying to learn 22 complicated lectures in 2.5 days… eek!

has just finished his third essay, two more to go. Kill me now!

is over this essay… and has barely done any of it.

needs someone to do his macro assignment! I have got no idea!

can't be bothered with these damn assignments and is thinking about what to write…

had a rare study-free weekend, but she reckons she has earned it!

is peed off after spending four hours in the IRC doing presentation stuff, saving it, going home and opening his laptop again to find he obviously hadn't saved the changes!

has four major assignments due on Tuesday… and feels like shit.

has never taken so long to write 400 words… and still has 3,100 more to go…

is drowning in a sea of work that she should have done on the weekend but didn't.

has had four hours sleep and is trying to pull 700 more words out of nowhere…

hates assignments and anything which could be mistaken for an assignment.

is writing another 15 page paper - hopefully the last paper she will ever write.

has postponed her essay to watch videos of The Specials.

is already sick of the assignment she hasn't even started yet…

does not understand anything to do with Chemistry and is in so much trouble with her parents.

is doing Uni, what else! 5,943 words and counting…

would do terrible things to get out of this essay.

is heading into Uni to hand in her last assignment, and has six days of school left! Whoop Whoop!

has only has five hours and 25 minutes of exams left.

is dreading going back to London because that means stupid study…

should be revising for a Spanish exam but is watching David Icke Youtube clips instead - much more fun.

is thanking Dennis for his brilliant advice about appropriate exam attire!

wonders are exams really necessary.

didn't realise that tomorrow's test and the 24 hour assignment are worth so much of her grade - not really looking forward to them now!

is going into academic hibernation… burrow!

is back in Newcastle which means I can no longer put off studying for exams.

had, she thinks, too much Vodka and is now wishing she stayed home and studied and not got drunk!

is attempting to learn my driver theory, and looking forward to my driving test…

is happy, happy, happy… except then I think of the exams I still haven't started studying for! Ooops.

is looking forward to everyone finishing their exams so we can go out.

is not looking forward to a long weekend of take home exams!

is starting to stress about this damn Italian exam… eek… non sono pronto.

is frothing on his exam timetable.

has Spanish writing tomorrow—going to fail, yet still choosing to do higher, all for jokes =]

is a study zombie, but only four days left… I'm in love.

is revising and hates it, what a boring thing to do with your time, we could be watching telly.

wants this stupid ass assignment to be done… so pumped Friday is here!

is on exams for the next three days—Great!

officially hates studying Health Behaviour!

is studying, studying, studying as he has nine more exams to go!

has a test tonight on Emergency and Rescue and if I pass I'm going to get paralytic.

is about to start preparation for her next exam in four days… I can do this!

is 4,000 words down, 8,500 to go… then she will have finished Uni forever!

is tired and is not looking forward to his BA and LGV exams tomorrow.

has four exams in four days starting tomorrow… FUCK…

is over study and feeling sick, whilst trying to revise for English and Drama :(

hit the last exam one time, like BOOM…

loves Consumer Behaviour and is super excited about the exam on Tuesday… NOT!

is thinking you are having a f**king laugh! Four exams in one week!?

is so angry that she will be studying for an exam on her birthday!

is just realising exactly how much she doesn't know about this next exam…

has handed in her dissertation! WOOHOO! Just five exams to go.

is realising that he has an Accounting exam tomorrow and appears to have done no revision whatsoever.

's head is stuck in a book in serious study mode… and is literally tied to the chair.

has been in Starbucks all day drinking Fraps and studying :)

is so, so ready for Uni to be over.

is saying congratulations to all her people who have FINISHED... she will be joining you soon!

can't wait for Thursday to be over, and finish my exam... so I can be drinking with Annie!

has one and a half weeks left of study... then holidays... woohoo!

is wishing everyone would hurry home from University and let's get the summer started!

never has to go back to Uni ever... but still has 11,500 words to write! Gggrrr.

doesn't want to have to take those exams again.

just sat my last exam... went better than I expected, but all will be revealed in July (so fingers crossed).

doesn't want to do it all again...

is pissed he has to do re-sits! Fucking space-cadet!

thinks she may have just finished her dissertation...

will be so happy after tomorrow because I'll never have to do Understanding Health again.

is hours away from finishing her study and beginning her well deserved holidays.

thinks she passed, but how well, who knows?

is getting pissed off that everyone at U.U. Magee is getting their results except for the F'n School of Law!

is ready to take on finals week and then graduation.

is less than 24 hours away from becoming a "graduate"...

bloody passed first year and is finished with school. Yeeoowh!

has passed her driving test. Third time lucky!

is now a fully qualified gym instructor and personal trainer! Woohoo!

isn't a student anymore.

is now qualified and has a Masters Degree in Applied Spanish Linguistics.

has won the certificate of high achievement in Industry Training Tourism Award! Jippi!

is no longer a student and is going to miss Uni. Yes, you heard me!

just arrived on the Gold Coast to celebrate graduating from flight school. I'm a hostess!

is now a "real" lawyer...

has finally completed my last essay for the year! Next subjects: Alcohol, fun and men!

is living for the weekend

is really up for this weekend... one million screaming Gays (that's 500,000 lesbians) outside my front door... mm er... should be good!

is excited and looking forward to St Patrick's weekend!

is counting down to Friday.

is looking forward to a three family day piss up this weekend but hopes there is no cross dressing involved!

is going to Melbourne for the Grand Prix on Sunday!

is getting ready for the North West 200 racing this weekend! Camping and drinking... my style!

is gearing up for yet another messy Friday night! Even though it's still Tuesday!

is very glad Friday has come round again and is looking forward to spending next Friday back in the UK!

is prepared for Saturday!

is actually going be participating in the Mardi Gras parade on Saturday, dressed as a handbag on the Thunderbirds themed float - Don't ask! Nervous? Yes!

is off to Bonds Uni on Friday to see the girls, it is going to get wild.

is heading to the A&P show this weekend...

is glad its Friday tomorrow for the girlie horse riding day in the Blue Mountains! Ooh what a laugh it will be with our little horse stories! Hee hee!

is so, so, so up for this weekend... and the next one... and the next one...

is warming up for Futuremusic festival... canie wait...!

is in Newcastle... then the Scottish islands next week... who's interested because I'm sorting out places?

is ready to rock the bank holiday weekend, cos the boys are back in town!

is excited for Pete and Eliza's visit this weekend!

is so tired and back off too work! No play until Saturdays Mardi Gras!

can't wait for the Fringe to start in Adelaide next weekend. Yay.

is awaiting a weekend of madness with Miss Lee coming to stay, whilst Niamh is off down the slopes!

is looking forward to the weekend... let's go army, don't hold back!

loves life again... can't wait for the weekend.

is having a pants party and cannot wait to see her mates on Saturday!

is going X-country Quad biking in the morning, but first there is the small matter of a few Friday night beers to be had.

is preparing himself for the next few entertaining nights.

is moving in to his own place with the boys and is up for the crazy party that's going to go down on Friday!

is gonna have a wicked night with the girls…

is wondering if anyone is up for going out on Friday night. (I'm in Strabane, remember!)

can now finally be excited about the weekend!

is looking forward to seeing the girls this weekend, it's been far too long!

is very excited about Sinead's fancy dress party on Saturday!

wants to go out on Friday!

is back in the bush and is so excited for a messy weekend…

is very relieved to have survived one whole week at work - thank God it's Friday!

is so ready for this weekends events!

is saying its bank holiday weekend - so come in for a drink!

is shattered the weekend is over!

needs this week to go at a rather quick rate.

is going to win the lotto tonight and have a long weekend.

is recovered and is feeling BACK! Training hard, ready for another big weekend!

is thinking… is it Friday yet?!

is looking forward to the fishing trip this Friday… gonna be messy.

is gearing up for a weekend of looseness.

should be writing his report on the Atlantic Council but can't be arsed as its SATURDAY!

is going to see Christina and Rikke this weekend… fuck yeah :)

is going on a stag this weekend. Look out.

is once again going to Bundoran for the weekend, which means me and Hayley will be as lose as ever.

is going on a day out to Leeds Castle on Saturday - they've got a jousting tournament and everything.

is loving the fact that although it's Friday today it will be Saturday tomorrow.

is preparing for a quiet weekend!

is so ready for sumo wrestling and the beach party in Venice!

loves his Friday nights.

is getting ready for Queensday in Amsterdam this weekend with all the orange gadgets I can find…

can't wait to go away this weekend!

is gutted that the boys leave on Monday, but the leaving do will be a blast on Saturday night!

is thinking it is going to be carnage this weekend in Newcastle!

is well up for Saturday.

is so happy it's Friday and a wicked weekend is planned - love it!

is off to peachykeen to count the amazing cocktails that will flow down tonight!

is an avid supporter of the four day week. Fantastic.

thanks god it's Friday!

is so excited for the weekend - Sydney fashion show, Carolin's birthday night and flying to Perth—Love it!

says: 'it is Sunday so I want a BBQ'.

is screaming Whoop Whoop. Beach Reunion Friday... can't wait to do some old school garage groovin'...

is having that Friday feeling in Spades!

is bang on about Judgment Sundays tonight!

is in training for Saturday night!

is getting pumped for the weekend and Miss Mairead's return. Bring it on!

can't wait to go camping this weekend. Anyone interested let me know.

is going on a pub crawl tonight... lets get it on...

is off to the Gold Coast for the weekend.

is gonna dunkin douNuts this weekend as my boy Martin is in town for his leaving party. YES!

can't wait for the rest of this weekend! Let your celebrations begin!

is pumped for 'Champagne Friday'...

is desperately looking forward to seeing her little sister this weekend.

is looking forward to a Comox Cats and Jervis Jocks reunion at the weekend... all absentees will be missed!

shouts no more work, its party time.

is getting ready for Paul Strange @ Hed Kandi tonight! Sitting on a roof right now beering!

is feeling a bit of a mad one coming on tonight!

is getting dressed right up to the max for Saturday night... gonna be the Belle of the ball.

is so up for Golf Pro's and Tennis Ho's on Saturday! hee hee!

is thinking... thank f#ck it's Friday!

can't wait for this weekend... yes I'm going back to Malcesine.

is glad it's almost the weekend.

is very relieved it's finally Friday...

is getting ready for Boujis summer party.

is gonna have a naughty weekend with the Justin and Samantha... Woo Hoo!

is off the scale with excitement about Sunday.

is looking forward to 5pm Friday... when the drinking begins...

is so pleased it's Friday!

is hitting Birmingham, and painting the town RED all over again, this weekend.

is going hunting this weekend.

is hungry to gobble up the Red Rooster in Dream Team this weekend!

is so excited for this weekend! Harper here we come baby!

can't wait until Friday... it's gonna be big...

is having drinks at Barcode at 8pm tomorrow. I'd love to see everyone and everyone I love!

is on the lash tonight...

is looking forward to next weekend when she'll have the house all to herself. If only she could afford to live by herself all the time. Hhmmm...

is celebrating the passing of another year

says 30 years and 9 months ago a lot of my friend's folks were shagging. FACT.

is gonna get hammered for Jemma's birthday and have a dance off... it's gonna be a disco Vietnam!

is now 26 years old and not as dumb as he used to be!

had a lovely 21st and hopes everyone enjoyed themselves. Can everyone put their photos on a CD for me?

is having birthday cake, as it's my mum's birthday.

is going to buy Hannah a birthday present. Any ideas?

is gutted that I can't have a picnic for my birthday! Oh well... Happy Birthday all my fellow Virgo's.

would like to wish Susan happy birthday for Sunday.

thought it was so good seeing all my long time friends together on the weekend. Well done Luke! ;-)

is getting older but doesn't understand why…

has today just started feeling normal after the awesome weekend celebrating her 30th.

sings "happy birthday to Steve" *clap *clap.

has it right on the tip of my tongue… Happy birthday Alison you crazy shimmying hippy.

is sending Amy Richardson lots of birthday wishes.

would like to thank everyone who wished him happy birthday and for coming to his party.

is excited about Matthew's 21st tonight.

says: 'happy birthday beautiful Stacey! I love you to the moon and back…'

is going to McDonald's to have a Happy Meal to celebrate his 25th birthday!

had a wonderful time celebrating Emma's birthday today with hot pink balloons and delicious champagne!

is loving the fact she got some lovely Tiffany earrings for her birthday!

is saying well done to all the birthday wishes!

wants to thank everyone for wishing him a happy birthday!

had the best party EVER!

is wondering what to buy her brother for his 30th (and can't believe her 'little' brother will be 30!)

went to the Hardrock Cafe last night for Jesper's birthday, very nice.

likes that the Queen has a birthday… teehee!

says fuck you to everyone who didn't wish him a happy birthday… No, seriously, FUCK YOU!

wishes a beautiful friend happy birthday - miss you a million times over :-(

says thanks everyone for the birthday wishes, now he is going to sink a couple of coldies for you all.

is heading to Ouyen for the weekend for Eliza's 25th.

says happy birthday beautiful Katie… you will have to wait for your pineapple until I come home, haha.

loves the gossip from her birthday party!

has had an amazing week, thanks Morten, Magnus and Natalie, a birthday never to forget!

wants to thank everyone that made the effort to come all the way here, thanks heaps it was a great birthday.

is stoked with the HD he got for Coffee as his present today.

sends a big kiss and cuddle to the birthday girl Karen.

had the best birthday EVER! Thank you all of you for making such a huge effort with your outfits - I had a great night and I love you all.

is so excited about the skydive and going out for late birthday drunkenness.

says thank you to all her pals for the best birthday wishes. She spent part of the evening with Morrissey! ;-)

is very thankful for all her birthday messages, mmwhaaa.

has just bought the office cakes for her birthday... E-numbers ahoy!

is thanking God that he has blessed her to see 21 and is thanking everyone for the warm birthday wishes.

is looking forward to seeing her family and celebrating her 21st all over again...

has dragged out the birthday celebrations as long as he can... maybe time to stop. Can't keep up anymore.

is excited for birthday celebrations and the beach today!

only has so many ideas! So many damn birthdays at once!

loved last night's birthday celebrations! Although ate too many prawns and drank too much wine!

is exhausted after a 21st and an 80th. Now just the clean-up operation to go.

loved catching up with everyone that she hadn't seen in years at her birthday last night.

is looking forward to Nelson Mandela's 90th birthday on Friday.

is NOT hung-over after her birthday and loved eating sweets and playing with sparklers on the beach last night!

is just reminding you all

is letting you know it's my birthday in six days! OMG miss all you girls so much! Bust a groove on my birthday for me.

is excited about her birthday in four days.

is looking forward to Sex in the City, ribs and rumps and her birthday! What a great couple of weeks!

is happy as it's my birthday today yippee, hehehe.

wants to tell everyone to keep next Saturday open for her and Michelle's big birthday party!

is getting ready to celebrate his birthday.

is gonna be a QUARTER of a CENTURY old in one week! My good god, where does the time go?

is loving her Tiffany & Co. necklace! Only 16 days until one's birthday!

is 27 on Friday. What the hell is that all about?

is the birthday Girl :)

is really looking forward to her birthday on Friday... party, party, party!

can't wait to bring on the 10th and 11th, and party hardy for my 24th.

is 22 today hip hip hooray.

is bursting with excitement for the show, University ball and birthday escapades happening next week!

is celebrating his birthday with his much loved family this evening...

is preparing for the birthday weekend.

says: Friday the 13th everyone in Somerset, we need as many as we can fit in the joint, hehe - my 26th birthday party drinks are there, so come on over, it will be a good one.

is talking about the weather ... again!

is contemplating going back to England for a few days because it seems he may get a better tan there!

is wondering why when we seldom get a bank holiday, is the weather always shite?

is home and surprisingly loving the weather!

is praying for rain!

loves lightning and thunder, reminds him of how small we really are.

is confused about the term summer!?

is not liking the cold...

loves the rain that is here, but doesn't like it being dark at 3pm... too early for my liking!

is going to get very wet tonight.

is in London and not enjoying the weather :(

is getting ready for an early winter, it may even snow tomorrow.

is very cold, but thinks the rain we have been having is awesome.

was a butterfly for the night on Saturday, but is now exceedingly wet from cycling in the rain!

isn't too keen on playing horsies in the pouring rain!

has given up sunscreen and is getting quite a good tan.

is rain, rain f**king rain.

is trying to get rid of her essays to enjoy sunny London.

is craving a sun holiday…

is facing the fact that I will have to buy a jumper… and some shoes… winter is coming ;-(

is wondering what all this stupid earthquake craic is about… tell me!

is very cold, but thinks the rain we have been having is awesome.

says goodbye sun, hello rain.

is thinking this English weather is nice but not as nice as down under in Oz… I think I will have to start using the sunbed again.

is loving Irish weather.

is thinking the weather ain't too great in the afternoon's here. What a pity.

still can't wear my new shades because there is no sun :(

is praying for the sun!

is in the very rainy Vang Viang, northern Laos. Where's the sunshine gone?

is going to have to walk to work in the rain. Boo hiss.

is here on Sunday, rainy Sunday.

is wishing he was on the beach… what a day…

is in the U.K. and it is cold! Oh, yes it is!

is braving the rain.

is not impressed with the clouds in Cairns.

is so over this snow.

is loving the beautiful weather and heat. And the fact he can spend all his weekends at the beach as well!

is happily sun-burnt after a sunny Belfast weekend!

is in Antwerp, its sunny!

is not happy at having to trail round Manchester in the rain!

is listening to the rain, spooning with Michaela and watching diaries…

is not impressed with the weather!

is wishing for nice sunny weather! Rain, rain go away!

is in Sydney and not too happy about the rain.

is so cold that she's thinking of putting her ski jacket on…

is wishing she was still in sunny Dublin.

is enjoying the sunshine.

would like the sun to come back.

is not getting to skydive in New Zealand - Fucking weather!

is enjoying gorgeous Melbourne weather.

is glad to see the sun back.

is wondering why the tropical storms keep following her?

is stuck in Port Blair because of Cyclone Nargis (not as rough here though).

is done with winter.

is finally in Laos but sitting in an Internet cafe staring miserably at the torrential rain.

is wondering why he went to Portugal, the weather is crap!

is surprised how shitty the weather is...

is not loving the cold!

is loving the weather these days... keep the sun coming please!

is in need of more sun!

would love a week in the sun right now... even the Irish sun!

is laughing at all the wet people that got caught in the rain...

is praying for fine weather for sports day.

is scared about the cold weather she is headed for!

is going to become an Expedition Leader, so please no rain this weekend...

is freezing, hurry up spring and then summer.

is not sure about the weather.

is loving Vietnam even if it is bloody cold!

is amazed it's snowing after the high 60's yesterday!

is ridiculously cold especially as it is so hot outside.

is back at Beverley but hasn't been to work since Friday because it has been raining and it has been too wet to go to work.

is more than a little confused at the moment

is searching for her inner 'ness' and dishing out seven different kinds of smoke.

is wondering if the A-Team are still on the run from the FBI?

is in an alter-ego called Sander/Jonas.

can't figure out the spiral binding in my diary... it just keeps on unwinding itself... I have big things to worry about, you see. Do you?

is babble... you know, like camel.

is loving the prospect of a four day week, its a Tuesday that feels like a Wednesday but is really only Tuesday...

is so bad, how bad is bad, bad is good and dawn is bad!

"pie-PO... pie-PO... pie-PO."

has just seen a man with the head of a chicken.

is scattered like fuck! Weeehooo mad Monday! Even thought its Sunday.

wants to apologise to the snail that was sleeping on her doorstep last night. It was dark, I never saw you.

is a cape wearing Youtube mixer.

has just spent half an hour hiding in a wardrobe from Bin Laden!

is like a rubix cube... I could sit and try to unravel the enigma of a girl but after hours of hard work I wouldn't emerge triumphant.

is going to stop working, dating, and being social to focus on improving my Sing Star skills.

is not for sale!

stood on a stranger at Hyde Park today at her request (I think).

is blaming her stylist for not living off the grid.

= La Da Daaa Da... La Da Daaa Da... Heeeaaay! Goodbye!

is "blink and you've missed him."

says: 'free mahi mahi, free mahi mahi, if you will, then gravity snatched the poor boy from his perch...'

is in woop woop state and what the fuck now...

is the immortal chosen one—now let the games begin!

knows that Elvis is still alive. Otherwise she doesn't know why they are in Memphis.

is a zipping goddess.

is making her debut as Porcelain doll.

is saying don't think that I have been unfaithful with my single life please...

is wondering... wandering and lost...

has just stolen a Hummer and is now prowling the streets looking for a hooker (GTAIV is the bollocks).

is not in any land at all because she's really confused...

is trying to find out if replacing water with protein is good for your health?

is... wouldn't you like too know!

is preparing the meat cleavers for Magaluf in three days. A few unfortunate females will be getting buried in the sand. Meat and shit!

is only hot when you can't see his ginger hair apparently.

found Jesus... at a Wal-Mart in Henderson.

is back to the place where the meat is white and raw.

wants him and you got him, not today Vicki haaa.

is alive in the grave.

loves the fact that Ashton Kutcher and I have webbed toes!

is a little bit crazy a little bit mad (in a Scottish accent).

can now officially spot a drunk - I've got a certificate and everything... may even do a little research later!

is pondering the complexities and consequences of asking an engaging question!

is the Leper Messiah...

just got caught up in some N.Y.P.D. shit!

is saying yada, yada, yada in a Canadian accent, and moving his hand in a way someone from Canadia would...

has too much hair on his head.

is turning Al-Qaeda... Bin Laden beard, Afghan in a bomb vest... Hit'em up, then look like a bomb threat.

wants to learn how to play the saw!

is hanging out with Santa and his good friend Jesus.

ate a big red candle.

is on the fucking run - lemme know if you got somewhere I can crash.

can't believe how fresh stay fresh lettuce is!

is five by five.

is death by carrot... fantastic... fantastic!

is visiting her parallel universe.

has never been traded for a washing machine… until now.

is Christ the Redeemer. Go in peace my children; your sins from the weekend have been forgiven!

is the winner of the phone-swimming-in-the-toilet game!

doesn't look left, doesn't look right… oh, nooo! Tyres screech! Everyone hoots! Bloody secret!

is back to her old trash bag ways…

is Adam and the Ants.

bbbbrrupp brup comets! Still laughing at Iris, the police and random gathering on her landing!

is a human Frank'n Being.

saw a hairless mouse in her loft!

is laughing, as he convinced Aisling to get him a Mars from the shops without moving, and without paying.

& Co. unwittingly dined in a restaurant-cum-brothel!

is yodel chum.

hAs StArteD tO RolL uP tHe hiLL…

is lost somewhere in the nervous system, between the brain and the spinal cord…

thinks backwards is aramat.

has a way that makes you feel so complicated.

is freaked that it is STILL Monday!

is contemplating thinking about thinking.

thinks equity is gay.

is a type of bra strap (according to urban dictionary).

is all about the same.

somehow got on a flight to Panama city, Panama… not Panama city, Florida… Oh my god I'm in Panama!

is smoking not to smoke about cigarettes.

is taking Robot to the pub.

is now reminded that humans just ain't that cool.

thinks Crowley is a fuckhead and people should stop calling "James"… its "James" it's me!

is off his nut pumping biggie feeling deep!

thinks that the greatest invention of mankind is… Snake II.

is letting the turtles get into the tomatoes.

got the chronic by the tree…

is probably going to lose her mind if another 12 year old hits on her...

is happy, yet quite sad =[

coo coo...coo coo...

is eating plum tomatoes on dry toast with salt, pepper and daddies ketchup because he's ever so hungry but he wants to be all full up, and wondering if this is the solution?

is not saying much

is constantly wondering.

feels like shit.

is on fire.

is generally undecided.

killed the dinosaurs.

is festively plump.

is over it.

is ridiculously bored!

is freezing cold.

is playing Solitaire.

is G.I. Jane!

is finally sorted.

is cooking lunch.

is gossip girl.

is burnt, oops.

is blown apart.

has chubby cheeks!

is bouncing along!

is loving curls.

has blue nails!

is checking again!
is Banksy... shhhhhh!
is carnaging it.
has lift off.
is stiff doors.
is officially home.
is Tip Top!
is Ellie's Flapper.
is injured again.
hhmmm Swedish candy...
is Googly Moogly!
is patiently waiting...
is writing music.
starts another week!
is... erghh men.
is watching Eurovision.
is an alcoholic.
needs new ribs.
is shitting herself!
is absolutely speechless!
hates scary movies.
is losing thousands...
is fading fast.
is sugar man...
is a mess.
is super peeved!
is at Lucyfallenface's.
is fucking you.
ate your cat.
's mobile is fucked.

says Merry Christmas.

is resting tonight!

is 38 degrees.

has felt better...

is still hopeful.

is feeling sticky...

is super fantastic.

is extremely frustrated.

can't stop smiling!

is in tears...

is racist... apparently.

is incredibly satisfied...

is so so...

is bitter sweet.

cleared her status.

is heaps good.

is off again!

is... not sure...

is 16.06.09.

is signature forever.

is slightly miserable.

is on it!

thought about it.

is slowly detoxing!

is long things.

is doubly blah!

is issue free!

likes those apples.

is car shopping.

is buying Strepsils.

hopes your joking?
is getting there...
is now happier.
is enjoying Kosovo.
is not telling!
is so confused...
is starting over.
loves Thursday rituals.
is missing something?
is mucking about.
is beyond tired!
Facebooked your mum.
is mud pie.
is selling clothes.
is being distracted.
is thinking 'FUCK'!
aims to please.
is feeling unlucky?
is almost free!
is going babysitting.
misses her visitor.
is still starving!
is too happy =]
dropped the f-bomb.
is shooting stars.
doesn't get it.
is stop loss.
has dancing tonight.
is jog on.
cant, just cant.

is actually Jo.

says 'fuck sake'.

is dreading Sunday.

is Captain Vortex.

is post-op.

is unpacking. S-l-o-w-l-y.

is becoming Japanese.

is the strangers.

is finished forever!

+ Tonje = Danger!

is looking mischievous.

goes sexual city…

is a matchmaker.

loves Emma Kearney.

is saying even less

is f@.

is tiny.

is puzzled.

says relax!

is pouting.

doubts it!

is fine.

is @co.uk.

is what?

has forgotten!

is blue.
says goodnight.
is recovering.
is praying!
is awake.
is... whatever!
is subliminal.
just is.
is ready!
is dove.
is drunk.
is trying.
isn't.
is hilarious!
is sore.
... sigh.
is fresh.
is mining.
is Sy.
is excellent.
is amazed.
is wanted.
tried it.
is shattered.
is v ;-)
feels sick!
is useless.
is broken.
is awful.
is wanting...

is POK-E-MON.

is stressed.

does...

is great!

is relieved.

is fantasmic.

is hypertensive!

is :(

is OK.

is Pillsbest.

is barn.

is indifferent.

wants to.

is chasing.

is done.

says hello.

is > u.

is hurting...

got freaky.

is suited.

allows things.

is Irish.

is planning...

giggles.

is in.

is pondering.

TGI Friday!

is 25.

is sunbathing!

can not.

is WTF?
smells…
is battling!
is b4 u.
is Atonement-ing.
knows alright!
is frothing…
will…
is ludicrous.
is day-dreaming.
saw him.
is rating!
is net.
is, maybe.
has graduated!
is beat.
is pooped!
is thinking…
is huuungover!
is awesome.
AKA God!
is on.
is smarzipan!
has impetigo!
is gay!
is hemma!
is chilled.
is Leeds.
would!
is doomed!

is buggered.

is amped.

is frozen...

is imagining.

has $.

is chillaxing

slept beautifully on new bed linen and king quilt... aahhh (said in the relaxing way).

is having a duvet day!

is hitting the tub.

is looking forward to sleeping and going to the cafe in the morning.

is returning herself to normal...

had a very chilled day.

is going to do fuck all... all day!

wants a bubble bath :)

is just chillaxing with my bitches' homie.

is like so whatever.

is gonna stay in bed all day and watch Top Gear and eat goodies!

is having a lovely lazy Sunday.

has spent most of the week chilling out back catching the rays... perfect bikini weather!

is trying to get a kitty to purr.

should be more worried.

is finally chillin'!

should really start tidying up before the others arrive... maybe just five more minutes... aaahhhh...

is just taking it easy...

is having a relaxed Sunday.

could do with a nice massage to accompany his day of relaxation.

is doing nothing ;-)

has a cuppa tea in one hand, his balls in the other, just watching the world go by…

is nonchalantly biding time.

kinda wants to hang-out in a chilled, low-key sense that doesn't involve town or money… any takers?

is gonna have a great lazy two days off.

is relaxing at home.

is going to take it easy for a while.

is having a night off tonight. Played mini golf today. I'm the best.

says karma: Relax.

is gonna have a lovely hot bath… hhmmm!

is doing nothing and loving it…

has been asleep for an ungodly amount of time… ah nice!

is a free spirit!

is going to make the best possible use of her only day off this week… by sleeping and reading all day!

is chilling after the weekend in the cosiest hostel… bliss.

is the opposite of stressed right now…

is mixing and chilling with friends—relaxing.

just kinda rocked up here, hey!

is loving lazy Sundays… especially knowing the mischief she will begetting up to later… and not having to work in the morning woo hoo!

is on the couch.

plans to chill out for a day or so.

is now home and relaxed.

is looking forward to chilling round Victoria's later.

has a beer in one hand, and his balls in the other, just watching the world go by.

is relaxing after the Sælbu Sumerfestival.

is taking it easy.

has just got home, put her sweats on and is about to snuggle into bed with a good DVD!

is now chilling… with Rodney and Delboy.

is doing fuck all!

is all relaxed after spending the day by the pool in LA with Ross O'Carroll Kelly - thus ending the literary drought which has been going on since 2001!

is loving the feeling of being all snuggled up in her PJ's :-)

is thinking with their belly

is dreaming of Bovril and honey.

is all Bounty'd out.

is devastated that the Queens Head is going to be sold! What will become of the Cajun chicken burger and Tuesday night beverages?

is saying lets eradicate coriander, its rubbish... while we're at it, Ben Daines too.

is thinking cuppa tea and hob nob's time!

is scooping the ice-cream.

is gonna eat muchas tapas... yummy!

is steaming a chicken, bland.

has a happy tummy.

is eating her first (and hopefully not last) Cadbury's Creme Egg of the season.

is finding this diet so incredibly hard.

can only stand back and marvel at the old mans pathetic eating habits.

is eating French toast... with Frenchy!

is not hungry for the first time in her life.

now has a coffee and a very extreme Italian shortbread! Thank you coffee fairy.

is wanting something sweet!

wishes the food would go down so she can eat more.

is at home eating frozen veggies.

has an egg with your name on it! That's for you Sofie.

is so proud of his baby avocado.

is loving Oreo's and milk... all at the same time.

has had success! Mmm tasty jam...

is making muffins!

had a fantastic and happy day. Feeding my friends ice cream and all.

is admiring Stacy Forbes, as she shares her love for marmite and marmalade on croissants.

can't get over the amazing coffee quality in South Africa.

is making pasta for lunch and Bridget is coming over to help me eat it.

is coming home for chicken soup!

is sitting on the couch while Simone cooks dinner.

says look... Marius fucking loves phenomlettes!

is making pumpkin soup.

wants more chocolate :)

is size 16 to 32 for some reason. LOVE CAKE!

is eating raisin toast and wondering why everything takes longer to do when you're late!

gets a Sunday roast lamb lunch today :)

is so full from dinner.

is heading over to Wilson's yard for a Barbie, but not before a jammy doh-nut.

's mouth is burning from all the chilli.

is cooking away a delicious chicken burger!

probably ate all of the cupcakes in the photo.

is going to go out for dinner tonight, stuff cooking it.

is having champagne and strawberries for breakfast and cider for lunch, tea and supper, Mmm!

is on Fruit Loops today.

is on a Maori night with the locals - and can't wait for the food.

is on the weekly sneaky six piece chicken tikka.

can't believe it's not butter.

is in bed and is hungry... as usual...

is having a fantastic buffet dinner right now!

is wondering where to go for dinner!

can not believe the size of the cow she attempted to eat last night!

is keen on eating some squid!

wonders if Jaffacakes are still low fat if you eat the whole packet?

is going to carve a chicken.

was dying just to ask for a taste.

is impressed with the chocolate, carrot and honey pudding!

can't actually wait for dinner and drinks with the girlies tonight!

is loving Carmel the provider of food in the IRC, hmm yummy milkshake!

wishes the whole world was made of raspberry liquorice... yum.

is very full from food.

has just had the yummiest dinner ever! Mmmm!

is thinking: Baguette? Croissant?

loves this cup of tea.

is going to make some yummy food with Silke today.

enjoyed his stir fry and fruit salad yesterday evening, with some excellent company again.

is wanting to eat and sleep!

is having fish fingers for tea. Fucking fantastic :)

is sick of cheese already.

is happy Marcela has gone to get coffee.

is thinking getting the best value for money at a sushi buffet is not the best idea he's had!

will have some freedom fries and a soda, yeah great, thanks.

is loving Smarties... the orange ones are orange flavour!

is eating another apple.

has eaten too much spinach and cottage cheese.

is sick after eating too many bon bons.

is repulsed by the peanut butter Beth is eating, eewww.

wants an ice cream.

is going to look pretty funny trying to eat corn on the cob... without any fucking teeth.

says you are making me hungry. You wouldn't like me when I am hungry.

is looking forward to eating a big Sunday carvery. Yummy yum.

thinks she may have eaten someone's brain for lunch yesterday.

is looking forward to the weekend shenanigans and my delectable quiche which is sitting in the oven.

has just had four shots of Vente Latte from Starbucks and is now wide awake.

is unsure if he's hungry.

cannot wait to eat a Twirl.

is waiting in eager anticipation for Johanna's taco pie from the oven. It's gonna be gooooood!

is going to walk the dog then drink some P.I.N.K. with Danielle.

thinks if only I had a lemon…

is wondering what she has to do to get some cold milk around here.

is making French onion soup with Caroline.

had a great game of tennis, which we followed with some fantastic duck and a double chocolate muffin.

is aching… yum yum… for some bacon… yum yum.

will never EVER give up chocolate again.

is eating one too many Jaffacakes… but I love them!

is enjoying freshly squeezed orange juice - Oh yes!

says to be fair, the salami and cheese are the most normal… the rest of Turin is fucked!

is craving for Krispy Kremes.

is back into oranges.

is going to make Turkish cheese rolls tomorrow…

is eating bacon and eggs for dinner.

just cooked some steaks, had a smoke and now he's got to get ready for worksies.

is bored and looking forward to having an Indian for dinner :)

is feeling sick from eating so many sweets.

doesn't know what to cook tonight.

is happy that caffeine can be found in concentrated amounts…

is loving his milk and two sugars.

is not having the most fun

cant believe that he turned up at my party with his new girlfriend!

is wondering who the arse hole is who stole her money, which she doesn't have much of anyway!

is far from being Oprah right now people!

will runaway with you.

is not gonna bother counting how many more.

is sick and tired of all her bullshit, but what can I do after coming all the way? Eerrrggghhhh!

has had the week from hell...

is saying I've missed you too Emma! Let the ear ache commence!

wants to live happily ever after...

is phone-less after a nice meeting with the MDP on the common.

wants out of here...

is dealing with micro organisms... this is not that much fun!

can't believe he did that to me, after everything I have done for him!

is gutted. Absol-fucking-lutely gutted!

just realised something very, very shocking... this is not good at all!

is the only gay in the village...!

is as married as a motherfucker!

cannot believe how disgusting some people are, that go to her school.

has now broken his fingers as well. Chore.

is pretty sure it's impossible to find a girlfriend in this city...

is thinking her day off could have gone a bit better... for starters her phone could have not just broken!

wants to know why people ask stupid questions!

is having the worst, most ridiculous day on record and its only 12:30...

isn't sure she's quite cut out for this.

has tonsillitis, on the fucking long weekend.

is anywhere but here.

hates Sods law. Wanna cry... again!

is going to bed feeling just as confident as he did a few hours ago... that's not very!

thinks she's ready to come home now.

is having one of those weeks, and can't believe some beatch stole her shoes!

wonders why people are so pathetic sometimes?!

is thinking this world is fucked up.

didn't think she'd ever want to be somewhere else but she does right now!

's manager has just took the jam from her doughnut!

is really hoping the right person moves in.

slept in a field last night with temperature at - 2, and happened to set up the tent on a cow pat... lovely!

is pissed off. Why do I let her treat me like that in front of her friends?

is wet, cold and bored... it's a winning combo.

thinks hospitals are a joke, she's been waiting ages!

is not playing Westbourne studios tomorrow. It's been cancelled!

is watching the clock...

thinks what a bunch of mugs! Pathetic people!

can't believe he is going to have to rip up his new bathroom because a tile came loose! Ggrrrr!

is in a really good mood. Let's see what will happen to change it!

was just told he's lost absolutely fucking everything off his laptop... gutted.

is going to get fit

is joining in a new fad called jogging, I think it's pronounced with a silent J, apparently all you do is run for an extended period of time!

is back from a hard gym session and will be chilling for the rest of the day.

is training for the Trailblazers 100km!

has begun her new healthy lifestyle, exercise is my new best friend!

is feeling virtuous having been to the gym this evening!

has just completed a crazy amount of push-ups and sit-ups before bed.

is going for a run. And is so thankful her working week is finally over!

joined the gym, done a spinning class and is fucked! Going to ache tomorrow!

is off to buy a bike today.

can't move… damn tone zone class!

is fighting fit after a morning walk to East Hammersmith and back…

is wondering now that I have an indoor heated pool and gym… does that mean I have to get fit?!

has just got back from the gym.

is going for a run as he really needs to get fit for this five-a-side tournament in Rotterdam.

is probably at the gym.

is after a brilliant weekend with her new sexy man, and just finished a two mile run which nearly killed her!

is not looking forward to running 8km in the Mother's Day Classic.

is starting a fitness regime!

is going to the gym for the first time ever tonight.

is just getting on his bike!

is pumped and exhausted from the gym!

is casually practicing her arm pumps for this weekend.

is joining a gym! Time to get back in shape… 'things' are starting to go south.

is loving 8am bank holiday Monday gym sessions.

is absolutely delighted with herself after completing the mini marathon yesterday.

is going on the treadmill… honestly.

is wondering if it's wise to do the London Triathlon given he can't swim more than about 100m!

is slacking in his marathon challenge.

has a sore toe after doing a half marathon! Oh yes people, it's the new me.

is off to the gym again soon…

ran for Wakefield hospice yesterday, running for breast cancer tomorrow, any more charities want a go?

is feeling good. This exercise thing really works!

is a true backpacker

has received a whopping $47 from his insurance company after having over $300 worth of stuff nicked. Silver lining... I am still insured for sky diving accidents.

is in the world heritage city of Luang Prabang, Laos just chilling out after four months on the road...

is sitting in a smoky Internet cafe at lake Eidir, Turkey.

can't believe that between Hannah and her, they've lost eight pairs of shoes, seven pairs of shades and a pair of bikini bottoms in three weeks.

is not happy with his hot water predicament!

should have picked up his lucky undies... then he wouldn't have lost his bank card on the second day of his six month trip through Africa!

is bus-statutionalised after 29 hours on board!

got so pissed in Sydney last night and has just realised, shit... I better go the airport!

is thinking 'why does my visa have to expire?' is going on a road trip with Gaby, Bianca, Andy and Anita to visit some rock formation or something!

is fed up with people trying to arrest her at airports!

is finally done with the washing after two weeks... no more testing the inside out and back to front theory!

is probably able to stay in Thailand three extra days, fingers crossed!

is second year visa-d

has escaped jail and is in Dunedin on a road trip with the girls. Exciting times coming up.

is finally in Copan after another ten hour journey.

is shocked to find out that Adam Air has had another crash. No wonder those flights were so cheap.

is a lil teeny weeny bit scared for her safety in South America.

is in La Ceiba after the longest bus journey ever.

is running riot in Liberty City.

is looking forward to Singapore tomorrow, where I will become an expert on Singapore Slings.

is sleeping in the airport tonight as the money situation is tight!

has one more night in the dorms.

is back in South Africa after three weeks on the road (and in a tent!) between Zanzibar and Victoria Falls...

is planning which way to go home in three months?

is in the Andes somewhere… and needs to stop checking out of places while still slightly intoxicated!

is very sad to be leaving Sydney but looking forward to doing some more traveling!

is camping in the rainforest, gonna live like an Abbo!

is wasting his trip on the Internet as it is raining - a little at least - damn you Mount Rushmore.

is off to Indonesia with $2.40 and one eye, oh the joy that is life!

is on holidays… not on the run!

is pondering the lack of pennies in Australia, but is excited for potential Lil Jenni visitations!

forgot how horrible jet-lag can be.

is heading home from Thailand in 11 hours, will miss my bessar mesa so much and to all backpackers enjoy the time you have left.

is saving money, by walking over Sydney Harbour Bridge instead of paying $189 to climb it.

is delighted she got her second year visa!

is traveling and surfing the eastern Australian coast in a Wicked campervan.

only has four weeks left fruit picking and then she has got her second year visa… wicked!

is fed up with eating rice and egg for every meal!

is trying to recover from her two day bus travel from Lao to Vietnam. Not Fun!

is in Gilligan's backpacker's and it's huge! It even has hot running water!

is the guy who took all the pillows!

is currently flying home on Saturday but is tempted to change it.

's traveling plans are going tits up! Ah well!

is alive! After hitching a lift and spending two hours in the back of a van with two men with machetes.

can't believe Caz and Co. are still famous in Utila. Sluts, capital S.

is a frequent flier, ha, as if!

is living the high life in Melbourne and very excited about the visit to Ramsey St.

is entering the wet T-shirt competition so she can get a few free beers. If you've got it flaunt it!

is depressed that she's only seen 8% of the world, when is she gonna find the time or the money to see the other 92%?

is living of salt and pepper sandwiches with McDonald's tomato ketchup.

is traveling towards Kalgoorlie now and his arm feels naked without a Side Bar stamp.

still has a passport. Fantastic.

is about to go get my sixth flight in two weeks… was a flashpacker for four weeks but now she is skint again… ah well, she is used to it!

is not loving Queenstown any longer, someone just nicked my jacket.

is still waiting for the AA man, the 'Love-bus' is in a bad way!

feels lost in a really big city.

is looking forward to moving out of the backpackers tomorrow… after 21 weeks!

is excited for the road trip today. She also baked cakes for the occasion, however certain individuals scoffed them. Sorry guys!

is in Christchurch and really should give his nuts a good old wash!

is on Phi Phi awaiting her new drinking buddies.

ended up skinny dipping at 4am at the beach in Brighton—shit, the English water is cold!

is in awe of the power of hot water.

is hoping his sisters tell his mum and dad he is skint and in Malaysia with no money and no phone, haha.

is loving Singapore… with 26 other people!

is really not loving the 26 bed dorm she is in :-(

has survived the 26 bed dorm! Next challenge… the night train to Kuala Lumpor!

is not looking forward to the overnight bus, yuck.

is very delayed at San Diego airport - but they have free tasting of shots in duty free :)

is going to Fraser island in the morning for three days. Get ready, I am going to rip up that 4x4 in the safari adventure.

is back in Brixton minus my luggage which they forgot to put on the next flight. I may be going out on tour on Tuesday with only jeans, t-shirt, hiking boots and phone.

says: can I borrow 3p please?

is leaving surf camp today, as he's doing the east coast with eight mates… the wild times have just started.

is in Santiago, misplaced UK SIM so only contactable by email!

hung out in a Bolivian prison today… as you do.

is in the West Bank. Don't tell my insurance company. Teehee!

has found the best place ever to live… hostel TV room!

is in Caye Caulker about to watch a private showing of a Croc show behind a dump in Belize.

is wondering who put a red plastic heart in his backpack!

is on a slow route south to collect Holly and Susan for a four week road trip before returning to Scotland!

is half way though his journey - six months gone - six months to go!

is living in the best hostel ever!

has now landed in China after a 50 hour train ride... Yippee!

is leaving Alice today to visit the rock after a brilliant four days in the middle of nowhere.

is gonna miss fruit-picking near Bundaberg, it's been the funniest month ever!

is looking forward to watching Neighbours in his campervan!

is chillin' wid de Rasta's in Belize man.

is in northern Laos, where after realising a cocktail costs the same as a meal and three nights accommodation... hasn't drunk in a week! A record?

is officially a hostel lifer... nine months and counting.

is nursing her bruises, cut knee but luckily not her dignity after a day out drinking and tubing in Vang Vieng, Laos.

is not on tour anymore, but traveling for six weeks to Chile and Colombia.

is off to Buenos Aires for the weekend... again!

is in scorching hot Laos looking forward to staying with some locals for the next few nights - just keep me away from the moonshine!

has been out walking around the streets of Del Rio, Texas all day naked, protesting at something or another. Must never waste an opportunity to get naked in public in a foreign country.

is actually enjoying the summer

is loving the beautiful weather and heat, as well as the fact he can spend all his weekends at the beach!

is sittin' in the mornin' sun, I'll be sittin' here when the evenin' come.

wonders is anybody out there feeling sunburned!?

is hoping the weather man is right about the heat wave tomorrow. Woo hoo.

is waiting for the sun to shine... come on...

is marveling at my redneck sunburn.

is counting her new freckles acquired over the sunny weekend.

is loving all this sun! But is sunburned :(

is hoping the air con is fixed tomorrow - its way too hot here! Looking forward to picnic in the sun though.

is pissed off she hasn't got a tan yet!

is sunbathing on a pebble beach in the 'hot' 22 degrees.

is loving London summer!

is hoping the weather keeps up! Thanks for the BBQ babe.

left her house for the first time this year without a jacket. Yay!

is burnt and peeling badly... sweet!

is loving the sunshine, but not loving the fact that her run of earlies starts tomorrow!

is enjoying the beautiful British summertime...

is so up for this! Summer is here, bring on the beer!

loves the sun and a thousand splendid sun rays.

is =[... summer =]

is taking care of his skin at Raiatea.

is unable to cope with the Perth heat. Freezer time, then shower time, then party time!

is mad about the sunshine.

is sunbathing! Crunk tonight!

is enjoying beach time!

is having fun, fun, fun in the sun, sun, sun.

is hating the summer, so many problems!

thinks 'Shirts off Sunday' is going to become somewhat of a tradition! Mostly in summer, I think!

is kinda perking up because its summer, init? Yeah!

is beating this heat with nothing but shorts on.

is wondering where the summer has gone.

is hoping this sun will keep shining all summer!

is off to get coated in sand.

is happy about the sun, and her two new Victoria's Secret bikinis.

is now beating the heat with nothing on.

is enjoying the sun and feeling nervous about tonight.

is in good humour because of the good weather.

is getting sweatier as the day goes on - air con broken again. Her arms have started sticking to the desk.

is celebrating Spring Break with some sexy Salsa.

is loving that summer time feeling.

is thinking how good this is: beers with my mates, while sitting around the BBQ in the lovely sunshine? It's good!

is announcing to the world...

is concerned his new short shorts are two short. Is it wrong for a testicle to pop out?

is bricking it ahead of his biggest opportunity to date. Will he rise to the challenge or will he lose his cool and fluff it up? Tune in next week.

is getting stupid, his IQ has dropped from 138 to 126...

does not fucking understand Hindu.

is speaking like an idiot after she decided it was a good idea to get her tongue pieced!

has a major crush on Sam Sparrow!

is cleaning his room again, as the bastard thing never stays clean.

wishes she could dance like the lil dude in the Drench ad... one day... one day.

is up an hour too early for work! Idiot!

is sleeping like its going out of fashion.

wishes she could ice skate in high school musical on ice!

is recovering after rolling the golf cart into the bunker!

needs a girlfriend... preferably blonde, 18—25, from the Nottingham area. Must be good looking and fit!

is enjoying the new addition to the O'Donoghe household. Mairead is not.

and Gemma Booth are heart breakers.

is shocked that they just raided a Meth' lab across the street from me. They seemed so nice!

... wanted dead or alive. Reward offered.

is being efficient with her time, as it is running out!

is wondering why Inia James keeps eyeballing his auntie Maria.

has been tattooed again...

is the newest member of the legendary Ex-Presidents... Coming to a bank near you soon!

is completely over morning sickness.

was back to her usual embarrassing self yesterday, smashing expensive crockery at yet another restaurant... cor can't take me anywhere, hehe.

is the only straight in the village...!

has an argumentative attitude when it comes to make-up and trance issues!

is going to win the lottery tonight - I can feel it in my pocket!

wonders if it's socially acceptable for a wedding speech to consist entirely of bald jokes?

is wondering how small is too small...?

was initially apprehensive about being Guinea pig to Greg's neck cracking, but has lived to tell the tale...

is having a baby GIRL!

saw penguins in Sydney harbour today... weird eh?

is an aunty again! Baby Tracey Mary was born, quite unexpectedly, at 10.42 last night!

hopes Heidi will be happy with what I've got her!

is asking the universe (and being very specific).

got locked out of his flat and almost brushed his teeth with something very unusual... looking forward to the simple life one day.

is boring

can't wait to meet Malcolm Turnbull at the next Lib's dinner, and thinks Labour will never get the budget and government expenditure right.

is wondering what sandwich should she have for lunch?

loves her new lights in the living room.

is going to IKEA later today.

has been queuing for seven hours...

is green... who knew!

is doing stuff this weekend.

is asking: 'Who would like to play Monopoly with me, it's really fun'!

has a very bad headache.

is so bored and needs something to do!

is learning the guitar.

asserts that, it's ridiculous in this era of globalisation and democracy that tyrannies still exist!

is well on her way.

is wanting to win the lottery.

is sat in watching TV with Shambrook on a Friday night. Hmm.

is up late! HEHEHE.

is downloading a free trial of graphic design software, trying to harness the designer within.

is nursing sore ribs… Eejit.

has officially switched my loyalty from United Airlines to Northwest Airlines.

is looking forward to going Wombat hunting!

is really hating flies!

loves hot water bottles.

is at home eating cheese and onion sandwiches.

is glad he shaved again!

didn't sleep so well, Naomi was wandering about the house all night…

is trying to decide what else he can Google. Any Ideas?

has just popped down to the shop.

is feeling like Hillary Clinton has lost her ever lovin' mind.

has a bitchin' new jacket!

is just sitting watching Coronation Street.

is a ginger-beard man!

has just woken up and is watching TV.

has a sore shoulder :-(

is going to bed… it's only fucking 9:45.

picked up a boiling hot pan today. That was not clever!

is watching the Bowls Championship.

is going to start drinking more water.

has gone for lunch.

is my middle name...

is better at Chess than you!

has driven a big truck today.

is not happy that her journey this morning took an hour and a half (usual time 45 minutes).

has a new favourite song...

's brain is straining.

has the same doctor as Harry Potter and Hermione Granger... how fucking cool is that?!

is happy with her new helmet...

is having a night off work. Boo Yah.

is waiting to see if his star sign this week will come true...

is going to be house sitting!

is wondering what colour scheme to use for his room?

is painting Laura's nails.

has resigned from the BBQ committee!

is counting the days away

is 62 days away from going around the World.

is just three days away from freedom!

can't wait. One week tomorrow until he leaves this dump behind. Thank fuck!

is at work... two more sleeps to go, then its Thailand!

is thinking 19 days until sun, sea and cocktails! Yippee :)

is counting down... two weeks until Ibiza! Yeah Baby!

has two weeks left before the trip to Spain. Can. Not. Wait.

is leaving Australia in less than 23 hours.

is focusing on travelling again. Three weeks to go!

can't wait for this shit week she's had to finish…

is leaving the helpdesk in two weeks.

is excited… only three hours until kick-off… Come on Reds!

will be in Toronto in 13 days.

is ready for eight days off and being back in South America.

is at work and is doing some serious clock watching… roll on half five, God damn it!

has three weeks to go, ooohh yeah.

is this time in three days, he will be on the plane to Lebanon.

is going to Cuba in two weeks and two days!

is skiing in two weeks, but where's all the snow!?

is counting down the days to Malia, only 27 to go…

is off to the US in one month and counting down!

is so happy to have booked his flight to Bangkok leaving on the 21st of June. Only nine more days of work.

has one day until the move… then its party, party, party!

is counting down the days until her adventure… 24 days until she leaves… Yippee!

is excited about going to Alicante in 12 days and only 21 days until I'm of to Turkey! Woop woop!

is five weeks out from departure. Life's a dream.

has only six more days left in Perth and then y'all gonna miss me like a sore head.

is wanting time to fly past.

has handed in her notice again, this time ready for the next adventure in four weeks time.

is less than three weeks from take off.

is on the edge of his seat, chewing on his finger nails . . . only 31 Days until the Pope is in the hood.

is wishing his life away as he wants it be July already!

is excited! Can almost start counting in hours now…

is maybe a little obsessed with popular culture...

is looking forward to the Sex and the City film next Wednesday... Cosmo anyone?!

can not believe she met Jonathan Reese-Myers and is seeing Taio Cruz tomorrow! This is way too much.

is looking forward to seeing Carl Barron tonight, and getting tips for my stand up shows.

loved PS, I love you, but it did make her cry.

is literally in shock that her favourite band (SNOW PATROL) are coming to Adelaide. Oh. My. God.

is still re-living the season four finale of Grey's Anatomy... Oh sooo good!

has watched too much ER...

is going to Belarus with Keith... but first there is the small matter of Sex and the City.

thinks that Threat Signal deserve some kind of fucking knighthood.

is listening to the Children of Bodom 'BloodDrunk' Album.

wants to be one of those BMX bandits, and take his BMX into a water park and go down the slide.

is off to Marion today to get his ticket for The Wombats.

has just rented the Rocky Legends box set as he is bored.

is counting down the days until she sees Sex and the City!

wonders if Dennis Lindberg is the new Hulk Hogan?

is loving Brothers & Sisters... I think I'm obsessed!

met Wolfgang Kahler, AKA Colonel Dietrict from Raiders of the Lost Ark! Nice one.

is going to see the PS, I love you movie! Yeah!

can't believe Jamie just got voted off Next Top Model. Devo.

is a huge fan of Goldclass cinema going... although not sure watching Indiana Jones was worth $100, thinking the Chronicles of Narnia would have been a better choice.

is excited to see Sex and the City and sip on Cosmopolitans... yum.

has been hanging out with his celeb' friends Johnny Knoxville, Hugh Heffner and Richard E. Grant in Hollywood!

is Gandalf the Greys' son.

just saw the new Indiana Jones film - not as good as the originals.

is watching Hell's Kitchen and having a great laugh! Chef Gordon Ramsay is a leg-end, you must see this!

thinks Mamma Mia is the best film ever! Loved it so much.

is giving Spielberg a C-. Steven you can do better, see me after class!

wants to know, does anyone want to come see the new Batman film with me?

is watching 300! "This... Is... Sparta."

loved the Australia movie! So good... but she now misses her girlfriends even more!

is staying at home with a DVD, but no popcorn or ice cream as its naughty! ;-(

is getting ready to have a girly movie night with... just myself—Oh how exciting! I hate being sick.

can't wait until tonight... wonder what she will see at the movies...?

is deeply disappointed by the latest Indiana Jones.

had an amazing day yesterday, and thinks Phantom of the Opera is amazing!

is back in love with Boyzone! Awesome night.

says Westlife: ab-so-lut-ly-fuck-ing-a-maz-ing.

is pissed off at how bad Indiana Jones was! Bring on the new Batman!

is seeing Fight Club tomorrow for the first time!

had the best night ever, sat front row at Croke Park. Lads thanks for the brilliant show, you were amazing!

is the Running Man.

thinks the Burn after Reading film is amazing! Good work Mr. Pitt.

is about to sit down to an Underbelly marathon!

would sell his Marge to see Daft Punk play live.

is happy to have found *This Is England* is on TV.

is watching Next Top Model tonight.

cannot accept that she is missing The Apprentice.

is so amazed by how incredible One Republic were live... she is missing them already, and can't wait for the next concert!

is listening to the Potbelleez! Oh the memories! Doooon't hoooold baaaaack, is there anybody out there...?

has just watched the Godfather for the first time ever...

isn't sure if he's looking forward to seeing Bon Jovi again on Wednesday night.

has felt the power of the Gladiators and is distinctly under whelmed. Bring back Fash!

is stoked she got Splendour tickets.

does not care about the new Sex and the City movie...

is going on a random road trip to Toronto to see Bob Sinclair! Can life get any better than this?!

watched the entire season four of Shameless last night... love it!

is going to see the Kooks!

is looking to swap Friday night Radiohead tickets (Malahide Castle) for Saturday night! Anyone wanna?

is sneaking into Splendour; he figures he did for Falls, so why not create tradition.

and Miller will be watching Underbelly II - Uncut of course!

is going to the Morcheeba gig on Saturday... Woo hoo!

who goes? Youuu decide...

is watching Minority Report.

... Stereophonics... Friday night... Yeah baby!

is super-pumped for the Say Anything sound check party... Loves it!

thinks Alex should be evicted on Friday! Grrr, get her out!

is happy that an albino is on Big Brother!

loved PS, I love you last night! Ribs n' rumps tomorrow! yum yum!

is watching Big Brother and I don't know why!?

loved Sex and the City and can't wait to get it on DVD!

is loving Ushers new tune "Wanna make love in this club." Just tell me where and when!

thinks Kris Kross will make you Jump Jump!

is going to see Mamma Mia finally... what a cure for a hangover!

thinks Dale in BB is BUFF!

is off to watch the Sex and the City movie tonight with her girls!

is gutted that Batman is over - I want more...

thoroughly enjoyed watching Rhianna get her umbrella out, she was excellent!

is Thunder, Thunder, THUNDER CATS HHOOOOOO!

had a good night at the O2 Arena watching Chris Rock! I don't care what Farrell says... he was funny!

is looking forward to seeing the Editors tomorrow night.

can't wait to go to the cinema on Thursday and see "Return of the Bun."

is deciding on whether to get a ticket for Electric Picnic? Emmm...

reckons that on a scale of one to awesome, the new Warren Miller snow ski film is right up there...

is just chilling with his close personal homie Billy Connolly.

personally thinks Shrek is god!

is happy that silly girl got voted out of big brother.

thinks Blood Diamond was awesome.

is so excited to see Hairspray tonight, and sing along!

wishes Alex would get voted off Next Top Model!

is on her way home tomorrow, and straight off to watch Mamma Mia, can't wait! Not long now Blaize...

is gutted that Prince has been cancelled.

lost his shite when he heard Infiltrator's new song! Get on board peeps!

is waiting for Desperate Housewives!

has just finished watching Narnia II—amazing.

is asking Desperate Housewives - what kind of crazy ending was that?

is trying to book tickets for Meatloaf!

can't wait for new Futurama tonight!

is being enthralled by Nighty Nights (TV) and enamoured by The Foals' Antidotes (CD).

is mourning the loss of Harold Bishop, an absolute legend.

is thinking this about the chips! She thinks you purposely burnt them to look like an airhead on TV.

is making an observation

is wondering why is lemon juice made with artificial flavour, and dishwashing liquid made with real lemons?

loves to watch her little brother sharpen his pencil with a knife as it makes him feel like a man! And also when he prods the fire with a stick... Ah bless him!

doesn't like that photo's don't disappear like drunken memories do!

thinks people should answer their phones more.

challenges you to look cool whilst picking up a Frisbee on the beach this weekend... it can't be done!

seen a lot of people that were on crutches today. Some days are just like that, but why?

wonders if anyone in Kentish Town has an IQ over 20... how do these people survive?!

still remembers that day a dog ran into our school. Everyone remembers that day!

is saying I have never been in love with Hollie.

knows that if you grew up in the 80's then you have entered the digits 55378008 into a calculator.

thinks wine is more diverse than whiskey...

wonders why at the end of every party is there always a girl with tears running down her face.

thinks there are too many empty bottles in the garden considering how many people were here last night.

is thinking life ain't that bad!

thinks it's just wrong... old women with mobile phones... it just looks wrong!

is amused how nobody ever dares to make cup-a-soup in a bowl, except him!

has his eyes on the road, his hands upon the wheel.

is not sure how Telstra stay in business!

has never ran out of salt... no one ever runs out of salt!

thinks the most embarrassing thing you can do in life: call your teacher mum or dad. He knows because he's been there.

is thinks Andreas Dahlgren needs more oxygen in his diving suit after making predictions like that!

wonders how accountants keep their sanity - must be the cash!?

is thinking that David Abrahams is the worst name ever.

does not know how he accumulated the 30 odd metal coat hangers in his wardrobe. Does anybody know where those things come from?

is amazed how well towels actually work...

never knows where to look when she is eating a banana.

wonders if the homeless man will return the favour when he's sleeping rough?!

thinks it weird that triangle sandwiches always taste better than rectangular ones!

is drinking in Murphy's and wondering if someone not from Strabane might come in?

thinks that you should always dump the top half of potential employee's applications in the bin, so to avoid employing unlucky people!

is wondering why does every bag of chips have a bad chip in it?

has turned into his dad. Today he put aside a thin piece of wood which he will use specifically to stir paint.

thinks the new Red Bull Coke is wrong diddly wrong wrong!

wears make up because it makes her look good!

has one question. Why would she buy something someone else wants to get rid off?

was out last night in The Empire, and the most awkward thing that can happen in a club is when your wine-to-toilet cycle gets synchronised with a complete stranger, and you have to keep talking to them!

thinks the most painful household incident is when you kick your little toe of the edge of the door.

knows that everyone loves the feeling of driving through a tunnel.

is wondering if a new car is the right thing to purchase when petrol costs $1.70?!

highly recommends the disgustation menu at Bennelong.

asks why do people who don't own a car, always slam car doors too hard?

misses decent Guinness.

got his head stuck today. There is no panic like the panic you momentarily feel when you've got your head stuck in something.

is confused as to why open plan offices are seen as a good thing?

wonders why Soapbox is like Parliament and takes a summer recess? Lazy fucking amateurs!

thinks it funny that all the ads he has seen for single people all have stunning girls posing for them! Are all the fat ugly ones now married and in relationships?

thinks it is hard to respect a man who carries a dog, unless it is wounded and over his shoulder.

wonders why when you have lost something do people always say "it was bound to be in the last place you look"? Well I'm not going to keep looking after I found it, am I?

is thirsty

is finally out of the office and tucking in to a giant glass (make that bottle) of vino! Happy days!

is happy, it's the tequila, tequila it makes me happy…

is going to turn into a Jäegerbomb!

needs time out and at least four boxes of goon!

is tired and wants a beer.

has knocked off and is now having a scotch.

is in a gin mood in Christchurch.

will have two beers, four Vodka's and six Whiskey's please.

is looking forward to Jäegerbombing with Mad Kevin!

needs a pint, sore ribs or not!

is about to try Pisco Sours, a local Chilean spirit!

needs beer.

is hoping Jesus will shout him beers for good behaviour.

has been gloriously reunited with tequila.

is loving the $2.50 beers! That's like just over a Pound! Rock on!

just turned 24 and loves Whiskey.

is thinking about red wine!

feels like a nice Cosmopolitan.

is going for beers in the George by Liverpool Street later if anyone is about, will be there from about 6pm.

will have a dubonnet with a twist.

is still frothing after an amazing win today, and needs to drink 28 bourbons at Gregg's 21st.

is going to take full advantage of the free bar.

is looking forward to a quiet beer tonight….

has just got up and is getting ready to go out on the beer!

is going to the bar, to buy a Sambucca!

has just invented the ultimate Jäegerbomb… involving eight shots of Jäeger, four cans of red bull, a jug and a midi glass… wicked!

is needing some anger management classes

hates smokers, and their attitude! Wankers!

is wanting a fucking MSN! What the fuck is it and why is everyone having cool abbreviations of their actual names…? I'm left out again—Wankers!

feels like ripping Brendan Byrne's sunnies off his head and throwing them against a brick wall.

is telling you guys to fuck off, I'm having a great hangover so don't bother me with your dumb Facebook apps!

is letting you all know what Ken told her last night "through no fault of your own... there will be moments when you may tumble short of his dreams". SHUT THE FUCK UP KEN!

is not interested in visiting the fucking cheese factory... what is it with fucking Germans!?

has decided its time for the truth... Colm, you are a fucking knob cheese!

is pissed off with his fucking Chav neighbour cunts!

hates people who use the word "stoked". Why is everyone suddenly so stoked? Just fuck off!

is in Queensland and hates how they talk!

thinks playing games is for amateurs, complete fucking lives is for the hard ballers...

is fucking sick of chavs... fucking silly fucks!

is apologising for the following strong language. I fucking hate thieving wankers!

says thanks people for tampering with his laptop! Whoever you cunts are, I'm going to fucking kill you!

is thinking I am going to rip off your face and wear it to the ugly ball.

thinks some people make me laugh! Who the hell do you think you are? They need to watch their mouths!

is gonna grab a knife by the blade and stab you with the fucking handle!

...I swear I wasn't kicking him... I was merely Riverdancing and he just got in the way!

thinks Johnny is a fucking fag whore and needs to cut his faggy hair and stop crying - you loser.

is starting to get wound up with people.

reckons if you want the leg room, say you want the leg room; don't blame the mechanism, you dickhead!

says... I'd love to stay and chat but you're a total bitch.

is telling you all to WAKE THE FUCK UP!

won't take no prisoners, won't spare no lives. Nobody's putting up a fight.

is so fucked off! Beware!

hates Madonna and Kylie, and doesn't care what all you Batty's think!

is pissed off with the lil children at Wake Up! Go home and get a job you pricks!

says 'Austrian bullshit secretive culture PISSES HIM OFF, why can't they just be more open? Fucking ridiculous.

is going to bash Pilko, the Faggot.

thinks Robert is a dirty tramp. She hates him!

is not your friend, go fuck yourself you fucking fucks... sorry bad language... I meant cunts... blow me!

is pissed that I have to work today and hates the fact that people are so fucking rude! So you can FUCK OFF! Bad day at work.

is letting you all know that my new email address is daniela@hotmail. Someone has taken my old one :-(Would love to kill those fucking hackeros.

is obviously losing their mind

is looking back to see if you're looking back at me to see me looking back at you…

has plans for this summer but is managing nix! There's spy's everywhere…

is pretty sure he just saw a midget run under his bed… that is not good.

woke up with the fear!

is holding his head in his hands—please, please make the voices stop… please, please, please…

is just informing you that the more you try to erase me then the more that I will appear.

is singing… "you find your demon's are your best friend"…

gave her mind away along time ago… it wasn't lost like some of you believe it was!

is Zuzana, just me and no one else!

had some really fucked up night terrors last night!

is having difficulties sleeping… maybe it's the fear of getting back to reality?

hates the dark evenings, as he knows there are people looking at him and laughing from the corners where the light doesn't shine.

is so head fucked it can't be real… can it?

knows… someday it'll all be over… I believe what I see when I'm asleep… we the people.

is talking to the little people inside his head once again.

wishes that people would stop turning into giant shorthand symbols.

is just not like normal people.

knows what you're doing… so stop it.

is going to beat them demons at their own game.

didn't lose his mine, it was mind to give away… I think?

is seeing things... she hopes!

always hears people say 'its mind over matter', but the mind is the matter, so how can it get over itself, when it is one and the same thing?

is... very slowly and painfully losing her mind, and it's their fault.

has lost his mind! Fucking onions and their bullshit.

is lalaalaaa one more lalaalaaa.

thinks night is often associated with danger and evil, because bandits and dangerous animals can be concealed by darkness. The belief in magic often includes the identity.

Facebook Facts

If you are reading this then you probably already have a good idea of how Facebook works and what it is about, so I am not going to go into that. Instead I did a quick search on Blackle and Wikipedia and within minutes I had gathered loads of information about the social networking site and its owners, revenues and so on. So if you are interested in a few random facts that I picked up from the aforementioned websites during August 2008 on how Facebook got to were it is now then read on.

1. Facebook founder and CEO

The CEO and founder of Facebook is 24 year old Mark Zuckerburg. Mark created Facebook with three of his friends from their University dorm room while attending Harvard University, and on 4 February 2004 Facebook was launched, but not to the world! Initially, website membership was limited to Harvard students, but was eventually expanded to include the students in other Ivy League colleges. It later expanded further to include any university student, then high school students, and, finally, to anyone over the age of 13. Originally located at thefacebook.com, the social networking site officially became Facebook.com in August 2005 when they purchased the web address for the sum of $200,000. The website's name originated in reference to the paper facebooks depicting members of campus communities that are given to incoming students, faculty, and staff in US colleges and preparatory schools as a way to get to know other people on campus.

2. The initial investor's

Peter Thiel, the American entrepreneur and co-founder of Pay Pal was the first person to invest in Facebook after recognising its huge potential, with the original investment in the social networking site said to be a sum around $500,000 in June 2004. The next company to take a chance and invest in Facebook was Accel Partners, who in May 2005 made an investment of $12.7 million, with Greylock Partners following that up with an investment of $27.5 million in Facebook in April 2006.

3. It's a LDN thing

London is Facebook's biggest city audience (bigger than New York, Paris, Tokyo, etc) and the UK with approximately 7 Million users at the time of writing is the third largest geographic in the system. Facebook, having overtaken main competitor MySpace in April 2008, attracted 132.1 million unique visitors in June 2008 making it the leading social networking site based on monthly unique visitors, compared to MySpace, which attracted 117.6 million (source: ComScore). However, in the United States, it has only 36 million users compared to MySpace's 73 million. According to Alexa, Facebook's ranking among all websites increased from 60th to 7th in terms of worldwide traffic, from September 2006 to September 2007, and is 5th at the time of writing. In a 2006 study conducted by Student Monitor, Facebook was ranked joint second (with beer, what else?) as the most popular thing among undergraduate college students, only ranking lower than the iPod.

4. Not everyone likes Facebook

It has been said that Syrian security forces were so concerned about a spam campaign that was using Facebook as a medium to promote false teaching about religion and war that they have totally banned Facebook! Apparently Iran has also banned Facebook, but when I was travelling through Tehran in autumn 2007, I managed to log on through the hotel lobby internet connection. Although a few minutes after I had logged off and moved away from the PC, a very serious looking man came in and checked around the area where the PC was situated before leaving again without saying a word. Coincidence? Maybe!

5. Investment by the rich and powerful

According to some sources it only took four years from its launch for Facebook to become the number one social networking site on the web. So with that in mind and after seeing a few other major players investing in Facebook, Microsoft proposed purchasing a 5% stake of the site in 2007, with it being reported that the offer was for up to $500 million for the investment. The owners of Facebook declined that offer, but on 24 October 2007 Microsoft finally announced that they had purchased 1.6% of Facebook shares for the sum of $246 million. Seeing that Facebook were willing to do business, Chinese business tycoon, Li Ka-shing (the world's 11th richest man) who likes to have his hand in a little bit of everything, decided he wanted a part in the social networking site and on 30 November 2007 invested $60 million dollars.

6. Facebook applications and users

As most people know, one of Facebook's biggest downfalls is the many applications that you are requested to sign up for in order to see who has hugged you, fancies you, or send you a request regarding something or another. According to a study that was done in November 2007 there where over Seven thousand applications with another 100 being added daily. Explains a lot, eh?! From around December 2007 to about the end of January 2008, Facebook had apparently seen its first drop in visitors in three years which was due mostly to the application spam within the site. Due to the fact that there are over 100 million active users on the site worldwide, market saturation may also be an issue.

7. Pictures

Most people with a Facebook profile will be aware of the amount of pictures their friends post in any given day, but did you know that daily number of photographs uploaded is over 14 million? Yes, 14 Million! Every day! That is a lot of cheesy smiles and drunken glazed eyes!

8. The potential Google and Yahoo buy-outs

Google and Yahoo could see the explosion in growth of Facebook users, and the increasing popularity of the social network sites, so in late September 2006 Yahoo entered into talks about the purchase of Facebook out right, where it is rumoured they offered $1 billion. Google later offered about $2 billion, but the Facebook owners where either holding out for more money or they realised they could make more in the long run from the site and decided to decline the offer from both sites. This lead to Mark Zuckerburg being nicknamed the "kid that turned down a Billion". It turned out to be the correct decision, as at the end of March 2008, Facebook had over 500 fulltime employees on their payroll and Facebook's internal valuation was around $8 billion based on their projected revenues of $1 billion by 2015. Not too bad for a program created as a school project by a guy in his dorm room.

9. Litigation

There has been an increasing number of court cases around this area recently, but one in particular caught my eye. On 24 July 2008 Grant Raphael was ordered by the High Court in London to pay £22,000 (about US $44,000) for breach of privacy and libel. Raphael had posted a fake profile page on Facebook purporting to be that of a former school friend and business colleague, Matthew Firsht, with whom Raphael had fallen out in 2000. This is the first time someone had been sued over a false entry on a social networking website, but in these Orwellian times it will probably not be the last.

10. The new approach

On 3 August 2008 the 'new Facebook' was launched with the purpose of reducing clutter, providing more control over how content appears on profile pages and showing the most recent and relevant content. It was a good idea in theory, but it caused outrage with users, with numerous anti-new Facebook groups being set up in protest. For a lot of people it was a case of 'if its not broke don't fix it' but a lot of others welcomed the new Facebook and its approach, as the result was that it did achieve its outlined objectives, and everyone´s Facebook experience was enhanced!

(Facts and figures sourced from Wikipedia and Blackle during August 2008)

Printed in the United Kingdom by
Lightning Source UK Ltd., Milton Keynes
141193UK00001B/40/P